AI Unplugged

Understanding AI's Impact on Our Daily Lives

Trevitt Hendricks

Table of Contents

AI Unplugged: Understanding AI's Impact on Our Daily Lives

by Trevitt Hendricks

Introduction

Y ou might be asking yourself: "What will AI really mean for my job or my daily life?" Trust me, many feel the same way. It's perfectly okay to have reservations about a technology that seems to rapidly change the world around us. Whether it's reading about robots taking over jobs or hearing about smart devices listening in on conversations, it's no wonder people approach AI with a bit of caution. We're constantly bombarded with futuristic scenarios and dramatic changes AI could bring, which can seem frightening. But take a deep breath—this book is here to guide you through these murky waters.

Think of this as a conversation between us, a chance to navigate the complexities of artificial intelligence together. You're not alone in feeling apprehensive or confused. In fact, your curiosity is the perfect starting point for this journey. The aim of this book is simple: educate and empower. We're here to turn what might seem like a labyrinth into something clear and digestible, while assuring you that AI can be a powerful ally if understood correctly.

Imagine this book as your intelligent companion, simplifying AI in a way that's accessible to everyone, regardless of your technical background. We'll break down the basics, explain the jargon, and explore the practical applications that directly impact our lives. By the time we're done, you'll have a solid foundation and newfound confidence to engage in conversations about AI's future impact and ethical use.

Let's start by outlining what you can expect to gain. We'll look at AI's origins, how it functions, and where it's being used today. You'll discover how it's woven itself into our daily routines, enhancing everything from healthcare to entertainment. Ever wondered how your phone seems to know exactly what you're thinking? Or how streaming services recommend just the right shows? These are examples of AI at work, and there's much more beneath the surface.

We'll also touch on how AI is shaping industries across the board. From finance to education, it's driving efficiencies and personalization at an unprecedented scale. As we unravel the mysteries of machine learning, neural networks, and algorithms, you'll see just how versatile and transformative AI can be.

But hang on tight, because AI isn't just a passing trend—it's an integral part of our future. The question isn't whether AI will be part of our lives, but rather how we can harness its potential to create a better tomorrow for ourselves and future generations. As we stand on the brink of a technological renaissance, the possibilities stretch as far as our imagination allows. This book will help you envision how you can play an active role in this evolution—be it in your workplace, community, or personal life.

Even so, it's crucial to remember that technology needs guiding principles. Our exploration doesn't shy away from addressing concerns about AI's implications. The dialogue surrounding AI is rich with diverse perspectives, whether they pertain to privacy, ethics, or socioeconomic impacts. Understanding these concerns is vital to ensure we advocate for responsible and thoughtful adoption. Your engagement and understanding will help us steer AI toward being a tool for good.

Imagine unlocking the potential to solve complex problems using a technology that processes data in ways we can only dream of. With AI, we're not just processing numbers; we're finding patterns, making predictions, and crafting solutions to challenges once deemed insurmountable. In sectors like healthcare, AI aids in diagnosing diseases, personalizing treatment plans, and even predicting health crises before they unfold. It holds similar promise across other fields, offering tools to innovate and enhance human capabilities.

A positive outlook is key. Viewing AI as a tool rather than a threat shifts our perspective toward growth and opportunity. This guide aims to empower you, shedding light on AI's benefits and demystifying its complexities. Together, we'll explore how it can significantly elevate our quality of life, opening doors to advancements we've only glimpsed on the horizon.

As we delve deeper into AI, remember that every step forward—every insightful discussion, innovative application, and ethical decision—begins with a foundation of knowledge. This book is your springboard, helping you leap into exciting territories with confidence and clarity. So let's embark on this journey, embracing both the challenges and triumphs that lie ahead, knowing that the adventure of AI is utterly worth exploring.

Chapter 1

The Dawn of Artificial Intelligence

A rtificial Intelligence, or AI, is a fascinating field that's becoming an integral part of our daily lives. Despite seeming like something out of a science fiction novel, AI technology is rooted in real-world applications and principles that have been developing for decades. From voice assistants on our smartphones to sophisticated algorithms used in industries, AI is weaving its way into the fabric of society. But how did this intriguing technology come to be, and what are the basics that make it tick? By looking back at AI's origins and understanding the fundamental ideas behind it, we can appreciate its potential and the ways it's already enhancing the world around us.

In this chapter, we'll take a journey through the early days of AI, exploring key historical milestones that helped shape the technology as we know it. We'll dive into the basic principles that underpin artificial intelligence, breaking down complex concepts into simple terms anyone can grasp. You'll discover how these foundational ideas are applied in various domains today, from analyzing data and understanding languages to making decisions without human interference. As we delve deeper, we'll also discuss the differences between AI, machine learning, and deep learning, clarifying how each plays a unique role in technological advancement. With this knowledge, you'll be better equipped to engage in conversations about AI's future impact and ethical use, whether you're curious, skeptical, or passionate about the possibilities it holds.

Definition and Scope of Artificial Intelligence

Artificial Intelligence, or AI for short, is a term that can often seem daunting or complex. However, at its core, AI is simply technology designed to simulate human intelligence. Imagine teaching a computer to think like a person does – this is the essence of AI. It's about creating systems that can perform tasks typically requiring human intelligence, such as understanding language, recognizing patterns, solving problems, and even making decisions.

The applications of AI are vast and immensely varied, stretching far beyond the common sci-fi portrayal of humanoid robots. In fact, one of AI's most profound impacts is in data analysis. Every day, immense amounts of information are generated, and AI helps make sense of it all. For example, businesses use AI for everything from predicting trends based on historical data to optimizing supply chains in real-time. Another exciting application is natural language processing (NLP), which allows computers to understand and respond to human language. This is what powers voice assistants like Siri or Alexa and enables machines to translate languages almost instantaneously.

Understanding the widespread presence of AI in our daily lives is crucial, especially because many people interact with it unknowingly. From personalized recommendations on streaming services to smart home devices adjusting your thermostat, AI plays a role. Even online customer service chats often have an AI working behind the scenes, ensuring users get quick and efficient responses.

To truly grasp AI's potential and implications, it's important to distinguish between AI, machine learning, and deep learning. These terms are often used interchangeably but actually refer to different concepts within the world of technology. AI is the overarching field, covering any attempt to mimic human intelligence functions. Machine learning is a subset of AI and focuses on the idea that systems can learn from data, identify patterns, and make decisions without being explicitly programmed for specific tasks. Think of it like a student who, after seeing enough examples, can recognize and categorize objects on their own.

Deep learning takes this idea a step further, using neural networks – inspired by the human brain's structure – to analyze various factors of input data and make decisions more autonomously. This is what allows for advanced image and speech recognition technologies. For instance, deep learning is behind the impressive accuracy of facial recognition systems and sophisticated language translation tools.

Exploring these differences can ground readers' understanding, opening doors to see the unique roles they play in technological advancements. AI might sound like a futuristic fantasy, yet it's deeply integrated into today's innovations, shaping everything from healthcare to entertainment.

To illustrate this further, consider the medical field. AI assists in diagnosing diseases faster than ever before. Through the analysis of medical images, for instance, AI can detect anomalies that might not be evident to the naked eye, thus enhancing accuracy and providing doctors with critical decision support. In financial sectors, AI algorithms forecast stock market trends and assess risks, helping investors make informed choices.

Education has also seen significant influence from AI, offering personalized learning experiences that adapt to individual students' needs. AI-driven software can identify areas where a student struggles and provide targeted resources to help them improve. This provides a more tailored educational journey, aligning closely with each learner's pace and style.

While there's undeniable excitement around AI's capabilities, it's equally important to acknowledge public concerns and skepticism. Some worry about privacy issues, job displacement, and ethical considerations regarding decision-making without human oversight. Addressing these concerns requires transparent dialogue and thoughtful integration of AI into society, focusing not just on its benefits but also on responsible usage.

As we move forward, fostering an open conversation about AI's role becomes essential. Lifelong learners and tech enthusiasts eager to engage in broader discussions about AI should focus on its development and future impact. Ethical questions, such as ensuring AI's decision-making processes remain unbiased and fair, need to be part of ongoing conversations about its deployment in various sectors.

This discussion should also highlight the balance between technological advancement and societal values, keeping in mind how AI could shape the workforce landscape and redefine skill sets needed for future jobs. Continuing education and adaptability will be pivotal for individuals looking to thrive in this changing environment.

Historical Milestones in AI Development

The journey into the world of artificial intelligence (AI) is both intriguing and transformative, shaped by a series of pivotal events that set the foundation for what AI has become today. One of the earliest significant concepts was the introduction of the Turing Test by Alan Turing in 1950. This test was designed to measure a machine's ability to exhibit behavior indistinguishable from that of a human. It opened up an entire realm of possibilities by challenging researchers to create machines that could think or act like humans. Essentially, it posed the question: Can machines display intelligent behavior equivalent to or indistinguishable from human thinking? The Turing Test became a benchmark, sparking debates on the nature of intelligence and laying the groundwork for future AI developments.

Moving along the timeline to 1956, we find ourselves at the Dartmouth Conference, a landmark event that marked the official emergence of AI as an academic discipline. It was at this conference that the term "artificial intelligence" was formally coined by John McCarthy, heralding a new era of scientific inquiry. The meeting brought together brilliant minds who envisioned a future where machines could mimic human intellect. This gathering wasn't just about discussing theoretical ideas; it was a crucible for innovation, where foundational concepts like symbolic reasoning and problem-solving were debated and developed.

Despite the initial enthusiasm, the road ahead for AI was far from smooth. The early decades witnessed a whirlwind of optimism but also faced significant challenges and setbacks. During the 1960s and 1970s, the field experienced what is often referred to as "AI winters," periods when progress stalled due to high expectations not being met. Funding dried up, and interest waned as the limitations of early AI systems became apparent. These systems lacked the computational power and data availability needed to achieve the ambitious goals set by pioneers. Researchers grappled with issues like natural language understanding and sensory perception, which proved more complex than anticipated.

However, these obstacles didn't spell the end but rather fueled further innovation and exploration. Over time, technology evolved, leading to significant breakthroughs that reignited interest in AI. The timeline of AI development is a fascinating narrative of continuous evolution, characterized by heated debates over core principles and technological advancements that have gradually bridged the gap between aspiration and reality. Breakthroughs in machine learning algorithms, enhanced processing capabilities, and the availability of vast datasets revolutionized AI during the late 20th and early 21st centuries.

For instance, the advent of neural networks in the 1980s, inspired by the human brain, marked a turning point. This approach facilitated pattern recognition and laid the groundwork for deep learning, a subset of machine learning that allows computers to learn directly from vast amounts of data. These advancements brought about a renaissance in AI research, transforming theoretical discussions into practical applications across various sectors.

Today, AI is woven intricately into the fabric of everyday life, from virtual assistants that understand and respond to spoken commands to recommendation systems that tailor content based on user preferences. The underlying debates that once seemed purely academic now shape how AI integrates into society, influencing decision-making processes and altering industries. Discussions around ethics and the potential consequences of AI are gaining prominence, adding layers of complexity to its trajectory.

The timeline of AI's development highlights not only technical achievements but also important philosophical questions about the nature of intelligence and the relationship between humans and machines. While early pioneers were driven by questions of feasibility, contemporary dialogues often revolve around ethical implications and societal impacts. The evolving story of AI thus reflects broader human concerns, transcending the boundaries of technology to touch on aspects of our identity and future.

Key Figures in AI Research and Theory

Alan Turing is often considered the father of artificial intelligence (AI) due to his groundbreaking contributions that laid the foundation for the field. In the mid-20th century, Turing proposed concepts that would later become central to AI development. His work during World War II on the Enigma machine demonstrated not only his brilliance in deciphering codes but also his ability to envision machines capable of performing complex tasks.

Turing's most notable idea was the concept of a "universal machine," which he introduced in his 1936 paper, "On Computable Numbers." This theoretical machine could mimic the operations of any other machine, essentially a precursor to modern-day computers. Turing's vision highlighted the potential for machines to simulate human thought processes, sowing the seeds for AI. Although his ideas were primarily theoretical at the time, they established a framework for future exploration into computing and artificial intelligence.

In addition to his theoretical work, Turing's introduction of the Turing Test has been pivotal in AI discussions. However, we'll explore its impact in other sections of the chapter. For now, it's important to understand that Turing's early exploration provided a blueprint many have followed. His pioneering insights encouraged scientists and engineers to push the boundaries of what machines could achieve. Without Turing's initial groundwork, the path toward developing intelligent systems might have taken a far different route.

Moving on to another seminal figure in AI, we encounter John McCarthy, who played a crucial role in transforming AI from a collection of speculative ideas into a recognized scientific discipline. McCarthy is best known for coining the term "artificial intelligence" itself. In 1956, McCarthy organized the Dartmouth Conference, a pivotal moment in AI history, as it marked the official birth of AI as an academic field. At this conference, leading researchers gathered to discuss the possibilities and implications of creating machines that could think like humans.

McCarthy's influence extended beyond nomenclature; he significantly contributed to the actualization of AI principles. He developed the Lisp programming language, designed specifically for AI research. Lisp's flexibility and adaptability made it a popular choice among AI researchers and allowed them to experiment with symbolic reasoning, an essential aspect of AI problem-solving. Moreover, McCarthy's emphasis on defining AI's goals and challenges provided a clear direction for researchers, fostering further advancements.

During his career, McCarthy was passionate about exploring the philosophical questions surrounding AI. He frequently debated the ethical and societal implications of intelligent machines, prompting others in the field to consider these issues seriously. His foresight in recognizing the broader impacts of AI technology affirmed the importance of cross-disciplinary collaboration in understanding AI's potential benefits and risks.

Together, Turing and McCarthy set the stage for future generations of researchers and developers. Their pioneering work created a ripple effect, inspiring countless others to enter the field and contribute their own innovations. As the chapter unfolds, it becomes evident that without the foundational work of individuals like Turing and McCarthy, many of the technological advancements we experience today might never have come to fruition.

It's essential to acknowledge how these early contributions laid the groundwork for modern AI, influencing fields as diverse as healthcare, finance, and entertainment. As we progress through the text, we'll see how subsequent developments are intrinsically linked to the visions of these early pioneers.

By examining the lives and achievements of figures like Alan Turing and John McCarthy, we can appreciate the remarkable journey AI has undertaken since its inception. Their innovative approaches and unyielding curiosity continue to be a source of inspiration, driving innovation and encouraging thoughtful discourse on the role of AI in our society.

The Evolution of AI Technology Over Decades

In the world of technology, artificial intelligence (AI) seems like a mystical realm, sparking both curiosity and apprehension. How did this fascinating field evolve from its humble beginnings to become an integral part of our lives? It's a journey marked by significant milestones and advancements that have shaped AI into what it is today.

Initially, AI emerged through simple algorithmic systems designed to perform specific tasks. These early systems were essentially rule-based, relying heavily on predefined instructions. However, they laid the groundwork for more sophisticated technologies. The 1970s witnessed the birth of expert systems, marking a pivotal moment in AI's evolution. Expert systems moved beyond basic algorithms, aiming to mimic human decision-making processes in narrow fields like medical diagnosis or financial forecasting. These systems used knowledge bases and inference rules to solve complex problems, showcasing technological progress in AI's capacity to execute specialized tasks.

Yet, as promising as expert systems were, they soon encountered limitations. They struggled to adapt to new information, and their rigid frameworks made scaling difficult. This exposed a need for more flexible and adaptive solutions in AI. Enter the era of machine learning. With the rise of machine learning, there was a paradigm shift from rule-based logic to data-driven approaches. Machines started learning from data, improving over time without explicit programming for every scenario. This capability allowed AI to move towards self-improvement, transitioning from being static systems to dynamic entities capable of evolving with experience.

A practical example of this transition is seen in how AI began handling language processing. Early systems relied on programmed language rules, whereas modern AI can now analyze vast datasets to understand nuances in communication, continually refining its responses based on user interactions. This adaptability is one of AI's defining features today and underscores its potential across various applications.

Advancements in AI highlight both its capabilities and limitations. While AI systems can process massive datasets at incredible speeds and learn from them, they remain constrained by their programming and the quality of data they are fed. Recognizing these boundaries is crucial, as it helps manage expectations around AI and guides responsible development. For instance, AI's ability to recognize patterns in large data sets doesn't necessarily imply understanding or consciousness. It's important to maintain clarity about what AI can and cannot do, ensuring that enthusiasm for the technology is matched with realistic perspectives.

Today, AI has seamlessly woven itself into the fabric of everyday life, demonstrating its practicality. From smart assistants like Siri and Alexa that respond to our queries to recommendation algorithms on streaming services shaping our entertainment choices, AI is everywhere. These applications not only simplify daily tasks but also personalize experiences, making interactions more efficient and enjoyable. Machine learning plays a key role here, enabling systems to learn from user behavior and preferences, offering tailored recommendations and insights. This level of customization marks a significant achievement, reflecting AI's progression from theoretical concepts to tangible benefits in our routines.

Moreover, machine learning's influence extends to more critical areas such as healthcare and finance, where AI aids in diagnostics, predictive analytics, and fraud detection. By analyzing complex datasets, AI provides insights that humans might overlook, enhancing decision-making processes in sectors vital to society's functioning.

As AI continues to develop, it's essential to appreciate the journey that brought us here. Understanding this trajectory not only demystifies AI but also highlights the ongoing challenges and potential it holds. For those skeptical or hesitant about AI, recognizing its gradual and deliberate growth reassures that while AI advances rapidly, it remains grounded in humanity's quest to augment capabilities, not replace them.

This exploration of AI's evolution encourages us to embrace its possibilities while remaining mindful of ethical considerations and limitations. It invites dialogue about the future roles AI will play and how we can harness its power responsibly. As we engage with AI in our lives, whether as curious learners, professionals, or skeptics, we're contributing to a narrative that blends innovation with awareness, driving AI's impact in constructive directions.

From Science Fiction to Reality: AI's Journey

From the early days of artificial intelligence, cultural perceptions have been shaped significantly by science fiction. Works like those of Isaac Asimov painted vivid images of AI, often portraying futuristic robots with human-like consciousness and emotions. These narratives not only entertained but also set expectations for what AI could achieve. In Asimov's stories, robots were more than machines; they had personalities, ethics, and sometimes even creativity. This colorful depiction pulled readers into a world where interacting with intelligent machines was as ordinary as talking to your neighbor.

However, while fascinating, these portrayals blurred the lines between reality and fantasy. People started expecting AI technology to replicate these fictional capabilities, leading to both anticipation and apprehension about its real-world possibilities. For instance, there was excitement about potential conveniences, like robots handling mundane tasks. Yet, alongside this optimism, there was fear about machines surpassing human control, a common theme in many sci-fi adventures. These dual perceptions impacted public opinion, driving both innovation and caution in AI development.

To navigate these complex narratives, it becomes crucial to distinguish between the allure of fiction and the practical realities of current AI technologies. While science fiction has opened up imaginations, the actual journey of AI is more incremental and nuanced. Today's AI, such as virtual assistants or chatbots, operates based on algorithms and data, focusing on specific tasks rather than possessing a broad understanding akin to human intelligence. It's crucial to acknowledge these limitations to set realistic expectations for what AI can contribute to our lives right now. By doing so, we shift from fantastical expectations to appreciating tangible advancements that enhance various facets of society, like healthcare, transportation, and communication.

A critical evaluation of AI narratives plays an essential role in bridging this gap between myth and technology. Rather than fearing AI because of dystopian tales or uncritical hype, examining these stories allows us to engage critically with their themes. This involves dissecting what makes AI characters in fiction captivating and considering how these attributes might translate—or fail to translate—into real technological outcomes. For example, the idea of a robot uprising reflects concerns about autonomy and control in AI systems. Through dialogue and analysis, such narratives invite discussions about ethical frameworks and safety measures necessary in developing AI responsibly.

Providing comparisons with specific fictional portrayals can offer relatable insights into AI realities. Consider how characters like HAL 9000 from "2001: A Space Odyssey" capture the imagination by showcasing sentient machines capable of independent thought and action. HAL's chilling presence serves as a metaphor for the uncertainty surrounding advanced AI decision-making processes. By contrasting HAL's abilities with existing AI technologies, which are predominantly rule-based and lack self-awareness, we highlight the progress that needs to be made and the safeguards required to address potential risks.

Moreover, using these fictional examples can demystify AI for those less familiar with technical details. Many adults, curious yet cautious about AI, can relate better to iconic pop culture references than abstract technical jargon. So, when discussing AI's potential impact, framing it within familiar fictional contexts fosters more accessible conversations. It encourages individuals across various backgrounds to engage thoughtfully in dialogues about AI's role today and its trajectory tomorrow. Engaging actively with these stories helps demystify AI, allowing individuals to grasp its capabilities and constraints without getting bogged down by technical complexities.

In essence, understanding AI's evolution through the lens of cultural media provides a meaningful context for discussing its current state and future directions. Narratives that once seemed purely imaginative now serve as conversation starters, prompting reflections on societal values, technological limits, and ethical considerations that define AI development today. By recognizing how far AI has come from the dreams of yesteryear, we can celebrate the milestones achieved and chart a course grounded in reality while still inspired by imagination.

Insights and Implications

AI is not just a concept confined to the pages of science fiction; it's a reality shaping our world. This chapter has walked you through AI's origins and its basic principles, breaking down what can seem like a complex topic into understandable pieces. From understanding how AI tries to emulate human thinking to recognizing the profound effects it has on everything from healthcare to customer service, we've explored AI's pervasive role in modern life. Whether helping doctors detect diseases or tailoring your favorite playlist, AI is everywhere—and sometimes, we're interacting with it without even realizing.

But as fascinating as AI's capabilities are, there are also important questions about privacy, job impacts, and ethical decision-making that we need to consider. This chapter encourages you to think critically about these issues while appreciating AI's benefits. It's all about balance: embracing what AI offers while being aware of its limitations and potential implications for society. So, whether you're curious about tech, skeptical of its intentions, or just eager to stay informed, there's plenty more to discuss as we journey through this ever-evolving field together.

Chapter 2

Demystifying AI Terminology

Navigating the world of artificial intelligence can often feel like wading through a sea of complex and unfamiliar terms. AI jargon such as machine learning, neural networks, and deep learning might initially sound intimidating, especially when wrapped in layers of technical explanations. But breaking down these terms into simpler language reveals that they are not as daunting as they seem. Just like learning any new skill, understanding AI terminology becomes easier once we start peeling back the layers of complexity.

In this chapter, we'll embark on a journey to demystify some of the most commonly used AI terminologies. We'll dive into the basics of machine learning, discussing how machines learn from data without needing explicit programming for each task. You'll find out how neural networks mimic the human brain, enabling computers to recognize patterns and make informed decisions. We will also explore deep learning, a powerful subset of machine learning that tackles complex datasets without manual feature extraction. Throughout our exploration, we'll touch upon the pivotal differences between AI and automation, highlighting their distinct roles in today's technological landscape. Additionally, we will address widespread misconceptions about AI's capabilities and potential impact, shedding light on both its transformative power and inherent limitations. Whether you're an AI skeptic, a curious learner, or someone eager to participate in tech discussions, this chapter is your gateway to decoding the elusive language of artificial intelligence.

Understanding Machine Learning

Machine learning might sound like a buzzword from sci-fi, but it's actually part of our everyday lives. At its core, machine learning is about teaching computers to learn from data instead of following explicit instructions written by humans. Imagine it as giving a computer access to lots of information and it figures out patterns or trends within that data. These patterns then help the computer make informed decisions or predictions without being directly programmed to do so.

Think about how your email inbox manages to filter out spam messages automatically. That's machine learning at work! Algorithms scan through countless emails to identify characteristics of unwanted messages, keeping those pesky spam emails away. Similarly, services like Netflix or Spotify use machine learning to recommend movies or songs you might enjoy based on your viewing or listening history. These systems analyze patterns in user behavior to suggest content tailored just for you, enhancing your experience with personalization.

Diving deeper, machine learning comes in different flavors depending on how data is processed—supervised, unsupervised, and reinforcement learning. Supervised learning involves training a model on a labeled dataset, which means each input has a known output. Think of it like teaching a child to recognize apples and oranges by showing them examples and telling them which is which. In contrast, unsupervised learning deals with unlabeled data and tries to find hidden patterns. It's akin to letting that child explore a fruit basket and notice how apples and oranges are naturally grouped without prior guidance. Then there's reinforcement learning, where an agent learns by trial and error, receiving rewards or penalties. It resembles how we learn by engaging with our environment, like a dog learning tricks for treats.

The success of these learning methods hinges considerably on the quality of the data provided. Garbage in, garbage out, as they say. If the data is riddled with errors or biases, the machine learning model's predictions will likely be inaccurate, leading to potential issues in practical applications. Therefore, ensuring clean, relevant, and diverse datasets is crucial in developing effective machine learning models. A well-trained model can recognize meaningful patterns and deliver remarkable results, while a poorly trained one might falter when it's needed most.

Exploring Neural Networks

Neural networks form the backbone of many AI technologies today, and understanding them is key to grasping how AI functions. Simply put, neural networks are computational models that simulate some aspects of the human brain. They identify patterns in data by imitating how the brain processes information. This might sound complex at first, but breaking it down helps us see its essence.

Imagine the brain as a web of neurons, each connecting and interacting to process information. Neural networks mimic this setup digitally. Instead of biological neurons, these networks use nodes or artificial neurons. Each node processes inputs and transmits outputs, creating a system that can learn and make informed decisions from the data fed into it.

A critical aspect of neural networks is their layered structure. Picture an assembly line where raw materials enter one end, go through several stages of transformation, and finally emerge as finished products. Similarly, neural networks consist of multiple layers—input, hidden, and output layers. The input layer is where the network receives initial data, like pixels of an image or text of a document. This data then passes through one or more hidden layers, which perform complex transformations. Finally, the processed data reaches the output layer, where predictions or decisions are made based on the learned patterns.

The beauty of neural networks lies in their ability to transform simple data into meaningful insights through these layers. However, getting a neural network to function well requires a thoughtful training process. Training involves a technique known as backpropagation, which sounds technical but is quite intuitive once understood. Backpropagation is akin to iteratively correcting mistakes during practice until you get it right. When a network makes a prediction, it evaluates how wrong or right it was and adjusts accordingly, refining its decision-making process over time. Think of it as teaching a child to recognize different animals; each mistake offers a chance to improve future guesses.

Technologies powered by neural networks are increasingly becoming part of our daily lives. Perhaps one of the most familiar applications is image recognition. Whenever you upload photos and your phone suggests who's in them, that's image recognition at work. The neural network has learned to identify faces and match them to names based on past data. Another everyday application is natural language processing (NLP), the technology behind voice assistants like Siri or Alexa. These systems understand and respond to spoken commands, thanks to neural networks trained to interpret human language nuances.

The use of neural networks extends beyond consumer tech and enters sophisticated fields like healthcare, where they assist in diagnosing diseases by analyzing medical images such as MRIs and X-rays. In finance, neural networks predict stock trends or detect fraudulent activities by recognizing unusual transaction patterns. Such diverse applications underscore the versatility and power of neural networks in solving real-world problems.

However, the journey of working with neural networks isn't without challenges. Training them demands substantial amounts of data and computational resources, which can be costly and time-consuming.

Moreover, ensuring that these networks produce reliable and unbiased outcomes remains a significant concern. Biases present in training data can lead to skewed predictions, reflecting inherent societal prejudices.

Despite these obstacles, the potential benefits of neural networks are immense. They're not just about automating tasks but enhancing human capabilities, enabling us to tackle complex issues in innovative ways. As we continue to refine these technologies, we open doors to even more possibilities, inviting continuous dialogue about their ethical implications and roles in our lives.

Defining Deep Learning

Deep learning is a fascinating and sophisticated subset of machine learning that plays a crucial role in the advancement of artificial intelligence. At its core, deep learning relies on multi-layered neural networks to execute complex tasks. These networks, drawing inspiration from the structure and function of the human brain, consist of layers of neurons that process data and learn patterns. Each layer is responsible for transforming input data into progressively abstract representations, which ultimately allow the system to make informed predictions or decisions.

One of the fundamental differences between deep learning and basic machine learning lies in how they handle feature extraction. Traditional machine learning models often require explicit programming or manual intervention to identify relevant features from raw data. In contrast, deep learning automates this process through its layered architecture. This capability to learn hierarchies of features makes deep learning particularly effective for handling complex data like images, audio, and text, where patterns are not easily discernible through conventional approaches. Essentially, each layer of the network builds upon the output of the previous one, progressively refining the understanding of the data until it reaches a high level of abstraction.

The applications of deep learning are vast and transformative, impacting numerous industries. One notable area is the development of autonomous vehicles. Deep learning algorithms power the perception systems of these vehicles, enabling them to recognize and interpret visual information from their surroundings. By analyzing data from cameras and sensors, deep learning models can identify obstacles, read traffic signs, and make split-second decisions necessary for safe navigation. Similarly, in healthcare, deep learning contributes to advanced diagnostics by identifying patterns in medical imaging, such as detecting early signs of diseases like cancer. These capabilities underscore the profound impact deep learning has across diverse fields, revolutionizing how we approach technology and problem-solving.

Despite its remarkable potential, deep learning faces challenges that highlight the current boundaries of technology. One significant hurdle is the enormous amount of data required to train effective deep learning models. Unlike traditional machine learning, where smaller datasets might suffice, deep learning thrives on vast amounts of data to identify and learn intricate patterns. Gathering such large datasets can be resource-intensive and raises concerns about privacy and data governance. Furthermore, deep learning models are computationally demanding, requiring substantial processing power and specialized hardware, such as GPUs, to perform efficiently. These demands often make implementing deep learning solutions costly, limiting their accessibility for smaller organizations or individual developers.

Moreover, while deep learning models have achieved impressive results, they remain susceptible to certain limitations. For instance, they can struggle with interpretability, meaning it is challenging to understand how and why a model arrived at a particular decision. This lack of transparency can hinder trust and pose ethical dilemmas, especially in critical applications like autonomous vehicles and healthcare, where potential mistakes could have severe consequences. Additionally, deep learning models are sensitive to biases present in the training data. If the dataset used to train a model contains biased information, the model may inadvertently perpetuate those biases, leading to unfair or inaccurate outcomes. Addressing these issues necessitates careful attention to data quality and bias mitigation during model development.

AI Versus Automation: Differences Explained

In our technology-driven world, two terms often come up in conversation: artificial intelligence (AI) and automation. While they might seem similar at first glance, understanding the differences between them can be enlightening. Let's dive into how these concepts vary, each playing distinct roles in modern technology environments.

At its core, AI is known for its complexity and ability to evolve over time. It's designed to recognize patterns, learn from data, and even make predictions. This adaptability sets it apart from traditional automation. Automation, on the other hand, executes repetitive tasks efficiently by following programmed instructions without deviation. Think about an assembly line in a car factory or a fixed-script chatbot that handles basic customer inquiries. These are straightforward applications of automation—tools performing prescriptive duties with precision but no room for variation.

Let's explore these automation examples further. An assembly line is the epitome of automation's role. Machines perform tasks repeatedly, creating parts or products without any decision-making involved. The automation script tells a machine to pick up a piece, put it together, and then move it along the line. Similarly, simple chatbots follow pre-coded responses to answer FAQs. If you've ever interacted with one, you know it feels like talking to a checklist rather than a person who understands context or nuance.

Unlike these static systems, AI thrives on flexibility. For example, think of AI-powered customer service agents. They go beyond just answering questions. They analyze your words, understand the sentiment behind them, and tailor responses accordingly. AI doesn't stick to a set path; it learns from new interactions and adjusts its responses over time. Another classic example is recommendation engines on streaming platforms like Netflix, which suggest shows based on viewing history—this adapting behavior relies on complex algorithms instead of rigid programs.

This distinction becomes more pronounced when considering how AI enhances everyday tasks. When employed effectively, AI can improve processes traditionally reliant on automation. Take predictive maintenance in manufacturing: AI forecasts when machines might fail based on various data points, allowing proactive repairs. This foresight reduces downtime and extends equipment life, something automation alone cannot achieve due to its lack of data analysis skills.

The intersection of AI and automation also highlights interesting synergies. Together, they create powerful solutions that neither could offer independently. Picture a smart warehouse where automated guided vehicles transport goods while AI manages inventory predictively. This symbiotic relationship ensures efficiency, leveraging automation's consistency alongside AI's cognitive capabilities.

The healthcare sector illustrates another compelling use case. Automated processes streamline routine tests and administrative documentation, minimizing errors and increasing throughput. Meanwhile, AI systems assist doctors by analyzing medical records to identify trends and recommend treatment plans, providing insights that drive better patient outcomes. Thus, automation takes care of the mundane, freeing up resources for AI to tackle more challenging issues.

Moreover, businesses today often integrate AI to enhance automated operations. Retailers have adopted self-checkout systems, automating payment processes. Yet, AI boosts this setup by detecting fraud patterns or offering personalized discounts, adding layers of sophistication to ordinary transactions. As machines grow smarter through AI integration, companies witness transformative impacts, driving efficiency while enhancing customer experiences.

To recap, AI and automation serve different purposes, although both are essential in technological landscapes. While automation excels at executing defined tasks precisely and repeatedly, AI's strength lies in its capacity to adapt, learn, and apply intelligence to solve intricate problems. It's important to appreciate their roles separately and collaboratively.

For those skeptical of AI or hesitant about diving into tech advancements, recognizing this distinction is crucial. The combination of AI's creativity and automation's reliability promises tremendous prospects without completely replacing human intervention. Instead, these tools empower individuals by handling monotonous chores while encouraging focus on innovation, creativity, and thoughtful decision-making.

Addressing Common Misconceptions About AI Terms

Let's take a moment to peel back the layers of confusion surrounding artificial intelligence (AI) and get straight to some basics. One common myth is that AI possesses sentience, or in other words, it has human-like awareness or consciousness. This isn't true. AI operates based on algorithms and data. It's like a sophisticated calculator—it can process information and generate results, but it's not thinking or feeling independently. Imagine using your phone to set an alarm; the phone doesn't understand time or have a sense of urgency. It's simply responding to a programmed command. The same principle applies to AI, no matter how complex its tasks might seem.

It's crucial to address another prevalent concern: the fear that AI will obliterate jobs, leaving humans without meaningful work. While it's true that AI can perform certain tasks faster or more efficiently than a person, it doesn't mean complete job extinction. Instead, AI often works as a tool to enhance human capabilities rather than replace them outright. Consider healthcare, where AI assists doctors by analyzing medical images faster, allowing more time for patient care and decision-making. In manufacturing, AI handles repetitive tasks, freeing humans to focus on innovation and creativity. Think of it this way; AI could be the co-worker who takes care of tedious tasks so you can focus on what truly matters in your role.

However, let's not pretend that AI is without flaws. A significant issue with AI systems stems from their reliance on data, which can be biased or insufficient. Since AI learns from data it is fed, inaccuracies or biases within that data can lead to skewed outcomes. For example, if an AI system designed to predict hiring suitability is trained only on data from previously hired candidates, it may inadvertently favor existing demographic patterns, potentially perpetuating bias. Efforts are ongoing to improve data collection and algorithm transparency, making sure AI becomes both fairer and more reliable. It's a reminder that, while powerful, AI systems require careful oversight and continuous refinement to ensure they operate with integrity.

Another mythworth debunking is the notion that all forms of AI pose a threat. Like any tool or technology, AI's impact largely depends on how it is used. Responsible development and deployment are keys to ensuring that AI benefits society without causing harm. Take autonomous vehicles, for instance. While there are risks associated with their use, when properly regulated and thoroughly tested, they could potentially reduce human error-related accidents, offering a safer driving experience. Similarly, AI chatbots, when designed with user privacy in mind, can streamline customer service without compromising personal information. Ultimately, acknowledging the breadth of AI applications allows us to embrace its potential positively while safeguarding against misuse.

Bringing It All Together

Wrapping up our exploration into artificial intelligence, we've dived into what makes it tick and how it's a part of our daily lives. From machine learning's role in keeping spam emails away to neural networks learning the faces of those dear to us in photos—AI is everywhere. We've broken down the complexities of deep learning and its stunning applications, from spotting diseases early in healthcare to steering autonomous vehicles safely. Alongside these, understanding the striking differences between AI and automation shows us where each shines brightest, whether it's in repetitive tasks or contexts requiring adaptability and learning.

Addressing common misconceptions helps demystify AI for everyone, showing that while powerful, it's not an all-knowing entity ready to take over jobs. Instead, AI supports and enhances human skills, helping us tackle bigger problems. Yet, we must tread with care as biases in data can lead to skewed results—a reminder that AI isn't flawless. The discussion doesn't end here, as AI continues evolving. Keeping conversations open about its possibilities and pitfalls ensures we're all ready to harness this incredible tool responsibly and ethically.

Chapter 3

The Mechanics Behind AI: How It Works

AI is becoming a big part of our world, and understanding how it works can be both fascinating and a bit overwhelming. You don't need to be an expert to grasp the basics, though. Think of AI like learning a new skill: it starts with tiny steps that build up into something impressive. The magic behind AI lies in how it handles data, learns from it, and then makes decisions based on what it has learned. It's like teaching a computer to see patterns and understand information just as we do. This chapter offers a glimpse into the mechanics driving these intelligent systems, giving you insight into how AI processes information and turns it into actions.

In this chapter, we'll break down the components that make AI tick. We'll explore how data serves as the essential fuel for AI engines and the ways algorithms act like blueprints guiding AI's decision-making. You'll also learn about the training process that AI systems undergo to recognize patterns and refine their abilities over time. By the end of the chapter, you'll have a solid foundation in the underlying mechanisms that allow AI to function effectively. Whether you're a curious learner, a skeptic seeking clarity, or someone looking to stay informed about technological advances, this chapter opens a window into the intriguing world of artificial intelligence.

Data as the Lifeblood of AI

In the vast realm of artificial intelligence (AI), data stands as the cornerstone, fueling the engine that powers machine learning. Imagine for a moment that you're assembling a complex puzzle without all the pieces. That's what it's like trying to develop AI without ample data. AI's ability to learn and make intelligent decisions hinges upon the breadth and depth of information it processes. Let's delve into how various aspects of data contribute to the vibrant and robust functioning of AI.

Different data types are akin to having a rich array of tools at one's disposal. Each type brings a unique perspective to the table for AI systems. For example, consider image data versus text data. An AI trained on images can learn to recognize objects, whereas input from textual data might enable it to comprehend language nuances. This variety lets AI not only enhance its capabilities but also molds it into systems that can tackle tasks across multiple domains. It's similar to teaching someone to drive different types of vehicles—they adapt their skills based on the vehicle's specific requirements. Moreover, audio data introduces AI to the world of sound, allowing it to differentiate between different musical instruments or identify voices. The diversity in data forms gives AI a holistic understanding, vital for tackling complex problems and offering multitier solutions.

Source diversity is another crucial facet when considering data's impact on AI. Just like a well-rounded education considers insights from numerous subjects, AI development benefits immensely from varied sources of data. Think about it; if an AI system only learns from one culture or environment, its adaptability becomes limited. By drawing information from diverse sources—different cultures, climates, or even social settings—AI systems become more adept at handling a range of real-world scenarios, making them more sensitive to global needs and challenges. Imagine a customer service bot used by companies worldwide. If it only understands Western cultural norms, interactions in Asian markets could be awkward or ineffective. Thus, ensuring varied sources is paramount for creating universally adaptive AI.

The quality of data cannot be overstated when discussing AI outputs. Consider data as the diet for AI; if it feeds on poor-quality data, its results could be skewed or unreliable. High-quality data ensures that AI delivers accurate predictions and trustworthy outputs, much like how good nutrition helps athletes perform at their peak. For instance, an AI tasked with predicting weather patterns requires precise and detailed meteorological data. Any inaccuracies or missing elements can lead to flawed forecasts, impacting industries and everyday citizens alike. Thus, investing in high-quality data translates directly to enhanced AI performance and reliability.

Diverse datasets further enrich AI's understanding, equipping it to handle nuanced and intricate situations. Picture a scenario where AI assists medical professionals in diagnosing diseases. With a dataset encompassing various symptoms, demographics, and case histories, the AI can offer more informed diagnoses. Such richness in data enables AI to distinguish subtle differences, which might otherwise be overlooked, and suggests the most appropriate treatment methods. In essence, diverse datasets act like experienced mentors guiding AI through complex decision-making processes. They provide context and nuance, enabling AI to operate with greater intuition and insight.

Processing Data for AI Systems

Data processing is one of the essential steps in preparing information for AI systems to work efficiently. The goal is to take raw data and clean it up so that it's useful for training AI models. Imagine trying to bake a cake with spoiled ingredients—no matter how great the recipe, the outcome wouldn't be favorable. Similarly, without pre-processing data, AI wouldn't perform optimally.

Pre-processing improves data cleanliness and usability. It's like tidying up your room before you have guests over. This means removing any irrelevant or missing data points, which could confuse the AI. For example, if an AI model is being trained on customer feedback to predict satisfaction levels, inconsistent entries or typos can lead to inaccurate predictions. Cleaning up these inconsistencies ensures the model interprets data accurately.

Let's talk about normalization and standardization. These techniques are key players in enhancing AI's understanding of data relationships. Normalization scales numerical values into a common range, like adjusting sound volume for consistency. If you're working with various datasets that measure height in centimeters and inches, normalization makes these measurements comparable. On the other hand, standardization transforms data so it has a mean of zero and a standard deviation of one. This method helps AI detect patterns more reliably, as it's not biased by varied data scales.

Understanding data processing can demystify AI's initial steps. Picture AI training as learning to ride a bike: data processing is akin to securing your helmet and checking the tires before setting out. Without this preparation, the journey is more challenging. Grasping these basics illuminates why AI requires such meticulous groundwork before diving into complex tasks.

The sheer volume of data available also impacts AI's performance. More data allows AI to recognize patterns more effectively, much like how exposure to diverse art styles sharpens an artist's eye for detail. When AI has access to vast amounts of information, it can make more accurate predictions. This is particularly evident in fields like healthcare, where AI analyzes thousands of medical records to identify disease trends or potential diagnoses.

Moreover, having a large dataset can reveal hidden insights and anomalies that might go unnoticed in smaller samples. Take weather forecasting, for instance: utilizing decades of climate data helps meteorologists predict future weather patterns with greater accuracy. Similarly, AI benefits from large, well-processed datasets by improving its decision-making capabilities.

Algorithms in AI

Algorithms are at the heart of AI systems, acting as the essential guides on how artificial intelligence interprets and applies data. Imagine algorithms as detailed instructions that tell AI systems what to do with all the information they absorb. Without these precise directives, even the most sophisticated AI would be aimless, lacking the capacity to make meaningful decisions or carry out complex tasks.

One might ask, why is selecting the right algorithm so crucial for AI? Picture this: each algorithm is like a different recipe for solving a problem. Just as using the correct recipe ensures a delicious meal, choosing the right algorithm determines whether an AI system will deliver the desired results. A poorly chosen algorithm can lead to errors, inefficiencies, and ultimately, dissatisfaction with AI performance. For instance, selecting an efficient search algorithm helps web browsers deliver relevant search results swiftly, enhancing user experience.

In real-time applications, such as autonomous driving, efficiency isn't just important—it's paramount. Self-driving cars must process vast amounts of data every second to navigate roads safely. The algorithms powering these vehicles need to assess variables like speed, obstacles, road conditions, and decision-making processes in real time. These demands require algorithms that are not only accurate but also lightning-fast, ensuring that every calculation is made instantaneously to guarantee passenger safety and vehicle reliability.

The role of algorithms extends to everyday internet use, too. Take search engines as an example. They employ specialized algorithms to sift through massive databases of information, quickly identifying and retrieving data based on user queries. This process involves not just looking up keywords, but understanding the context and relevance of the information requested. For a simple user query, countless algorithms work tirelessly behind the scenes to provide the most accurate and useful results within milliseconds.

It's worth noting that while algorithms have transformed AI into a powerful tool, their selection, implementation, and optimization require skill and insight. Every AI system's success depends significantly on how well its algorithms align with its intended purpose. Thus, understanding the nuances of algorithm selection becomes integral to harnessing AI's full potential. Matching the right algorithm to the task at hand is akin to fitting the perfect key into a lock—it opens doors to unprecedented possibilities and innovations.

For those new to understanding AI, it's helpful to appreciate the foundational role algorithms play. They're not just abstract concepts limited to tech-savvy experts; they're practical tools shaping how AI interacts with our world. By demystifying algorithms as fundamental components rather than intimidating complexities, we empower people to engage more confidently with AI technology. Whether through developing a basic comprehension of algorithm types or recognizing their implications in various innovations, everyone can take part in discussions about AI's future.

Furthermore, exploring algorithms offers insights into broader technological conversations. As algorithms evolve, so do AI capabilities, leading to groundbreaking advancements across industries. From healthcare, where algorithms assist in diagnosing diseases, to finance, where they forecast market trends, these tools are revolutionizing how tasks are approached and executed. Understanding algorithms allows individuals to appreciate not only the present state of AI but its incredible promise for the future.

Training AI Models

Training AI models is an intriguing process that essentially teaches machines to identify and understand patterns through exposure to data. Imagine trying to teach someone new how to play a musical instrument. You wouldn't merely hand them the instrument and expect instant proficiency. Instead, you'd progressively expose them to various musical notes, rhythms, and techniques until they start recognizing patterns and can eventually play melodies on their own. This is quite similar to how we train AI systems.

When we talk about training AI, we're often referring to supervised learning. This method relies heavily on labeled data, much like a teacher guiding a student with clear instructions. If you think about teaching a child the difference between cats and dogs, you'd show them various pictures of both animals, clearly labeling each one. Over time, with enough examples, the child learns to identify cats and dogs even in unfamiliar settings. In the case of AI, this labeled data serves as a reference point, helping the system to learn and make predictions based on what it has already encountered. By providing these cues, AI models gradually become adept at distinguishing between different inputs.

Data volume plays a critical role in AI's training success. Large datasets enable AI models to recognize broader patterns and avoid overfitting— where the model knows training data too well but struggles with new, unseen data. Think of overfitting like memorizing answers for a test; it might work in familiar situations but falls short when faced with slightly altered questions. By using extensive datasets, we ensure that our AI doesn't just memorize but genuinely understands the underlying patterns, allowing it to perform better in diverse scenarios.

Moreover, the diversity of the dataset enriches the AI's ability to discern complex patterns within the data. Picture preparing a chef who wishes to master international cuisine. Exposure to an array of ingredients and cooking techniques from around the world would provide a well-rounded skill set, enabling them to whip up dishes from various culinary traditions. Similarly, AI benefits from vast and varied datasets, allowing it to adapt to different contexts and challenges.

An important technique used to improve learning efficiency in AI is batch learning. Consider it like studying in manageable chunks rather than cramming all at once before a big exam. With batch learning, data is divided into small batches, and the model learns from these subsets over several iterations. It minimizes the strain on computational resources and typically results in more stable and accurate learning outcomes. The approach helps in streamlining the training process, making it efficient and effective without overwhelming the system with too much information simultaneously.

Batch learning is analogous to reading a lengthy novel one chapter at a time instead of attempting to digest it in a single sitting. Each section provides insights and development, contributing incrementally to overall understanding. For AI models, processing smaller batches at a time ensures a smoother progression and fine-tuning of pattern recognition capabilities.

However, one must not overlook the need for constant evaluation during training. It involves checking if the AI's predictions are matching actual outcomes or if adjustments are needed. Using validation data, separate from training data, allows us to monitor the performance objectively. If discrepancies surface, it signals a need for optimization, perhaps by tweaking the model's parameters or adjusting data balance.

Consider a scenario where a student practicing for a violin recital receives feedback on missed notes or improper rhythm. This critique helps the student adjust their practice regimen, ensuring they correct errors and improve performance. Feedback loops created during AI training function similarly, guiding the model towards greater accuracy and better predictions.

In the realm of AI training, ethical considerations also come into play. We must be cautious of biases in data that could lead to skewed AI decision-making. Careful curation and diversification of training data are necessary to mitigate such issues, ensuring outputs remain fair and unbiased.

To illustrate, imagine a fashion recommendation AI trained only on Western styles. Its suggestions would likely fail to resonate with users accustomed to Eastern fashion trends. A balanced dataset, representative of varied global fashion influences, would enable the AI to offer more universally appealing recommendations.

As AI models continue to evolve, so do the methods and strategies for training them. Adaptive learning techniques, inspired by biological neural networks, are paving the way for smarter, more flexible AI capable of self-improvement. While traditional supervised learning remains foundational, innovations are gradually propelling the field forward, opening new possibilities for AI applications in everyday life.

AI's Capacity for Pattern Recognition

Recognizing patterns is at the heart of what artificial intelligence (AI) does best. Just like how our brains are wired to see similarities and make connections, AI systems are designed to identify patterns in data that might not be immediately obvious to human analysts. This ability forms the backbone of many AI applications, guiding the machines to make informed conclusions and operate effectively across numerous tasks.

Take, for instance, the way AI handles pattern recognition. When AI scans through immense amounts of data, it looks for recurring themes or features. These might include similar items in a shopping database, repeated transactions in financial records, or even familiar faces in a crowd. By identifying these patterns, AI doesn't just store raw data; it processes this information to derive meaning, ultimately offering insights or predictions that hold significant value. This can mean detecting fraud by recognizing suspicious activity or identifying disease outbreaks before they escalate, showcasing AI's potential to revolutionize industries.

In the world of photography, pattern recognition finds another exciting application. Ever noticed how some apps can effortlessly group your holiday pictures into distinct albums featuring people, places, or pets? That's AI at work, categorizing images based on visual attributes like shapes, colors, or textures. This capability not only saves time but also enhances user experiences by ensuring that photos aren't just jumbled together with no order. For casual users, this means spending less time sorting photos manually and more time sharing memories. For photographers and digital artists, it offers a streamlined workflow, letting them focus on creativity rather than mundane organizational tasks.

However, AI's pattern recognition is not without its challenges. A primary obstacle arises from noise—unnecessary or irrelevant data that muddles the clarity of what's being analyzed. Noise can severely disrupt an AI's ability to recognize patterns accurately. Imagine trying to listen to a friend's voice in a crowded room; that's essentially what AI deals with when confronted with noisy data. To combat this, AI systems rely heavily on robust algorithms capable of filtering out unnecessary distractions while honing in on relevant signals. These algorithms are continually refined and updated to ensure their effectiveness in various environments, whether it's analyzing satellite images or monitoring social media trends.

The success of pattern recognition also largely depends on the quality and quantity of training the AI receives. Training is akin to education for humans; it's where AI learns to differentiate between what's important and what's not, sharpening its ability to pick out meaningful patterns amidst the clutter. It is during this phase that AI models are exposed to vast datasets that encompass a range of scenarios and conditions. Adequate training ensures that AI doesn't just memorize what it's been shown but instead develops the judgment to discern between relevant and irrelevant patterns in new, unseen data.

Without proper training, AI could easily become overconfident in its abilities, mistaking coincidences for consistent patterns. Contextual understanding plays a crucial role here; the more diverse and nuanced the training data, the better equipped the AI system is to handle real-world complexities. For example, training an AI in identifying emotional expressions would require a dataset rich with varied human interactions, capturing different cultural contexts and subtle facial cues to avoid misinterpretations.

One way AI has been successfully trained to improve its pattern recognition capabilities is through the use of supervised learning techniques. Here, AI models are guided by labeled examples, much like how students learn by reviewing textbooks and solving problems under supervision. This structured approach helps reinforce accurate pattern identification, boosting confidence in the AI's outputs. However, training isn't just about feeding algorithms heaps of data; it's about providing meaningful, well-annotated datasets that reflect the intricacies of the task at hand.

Moreover, AI's grasp of pattern recognition doesn't remain static. Continuous learning mechanisms allow AI systems to evolve by integrating new information over time. Much like how we grow by assimilating new knowledge and experiences, AI systems improve as they encounter fresh data sets. This adaptability is particularly vital in fast-paced industries such as cybersecurity, where threats are constantly evolving and require nimble responses from AI-powered systems.

Bringing It All Together

In this chapter, we've journeyed through the fascinating inner workings of AI systems, focusing on how they process data and utilize algorithms for learning. We've seen how crucial diverse and high-quality data is in shaping AI's abilities, helping these systems learn and make informed decisions. By dissecting various types of data like images, text, and audio, we've understood that each one adds unique value to AI, much like different tools in a toolbox. Our exploration into data processing showed us the importance of tidying up raw information so that AI can function at its best. This means cleaning, normalizing, and making sense of data before it's fed to AI models, ensuring they're well-prepared for their tasks.

As we delve deeper into the functionality of AI, it's clear how essential algorithms are in guiding these systems. Algorithms serve as the detailed instructions that allow AI to interpret and apply the processed data effectively. From self-driving cars to search engines, the right algorithm can make or break an AI's performance. While training AI models might sound complex, it follows a logic similar to teaching someone a new skill: with lots of examples and constant feedback. And finally, the magic of pattern recognition is what allows AI to identify trends and anomalies, transforming data into insights. This chapter has laid out the foundational elements of AI's core processes, offering a glimpse into how these intelligent systems operate and evolve.

Chapter 4

AI in Our Everyday Lives

A rtificial intelligence (AI) is quietly transforming our everyday lives, making things easier and more efficient in ways we might not even notice. From the moment you wake up to your favorite song, played by an AI-powered virtual assistant, to wrapping up your day with a smart home device that turns off lights automatically, AI is hard at work behind the scenes. These technologies seamlessly integrate into our daily tasks, offering unparalleled convenience and personalization. It's not just about fancy gadgets; it's about creating smoother, smarter routines that free up time for what really matters.

In this chapter, we'll dive into the specifics of how AI powers these experiences. We'll explore the role of virtual assistants like Siri or Alexa in managing tasks effortlessly, as well as how smart home devices enhance efficiency by learning from our routines. You'll also find out how AI tackles privacy concerns, ensuring safety without sacrificing convenience. By unpacking these elements, this chapter aims to shed light on both the practical benefits and potential concerns of integrating AI into our daily lives. Whether you're simply curious or a bit skeptical about AI's presence in your home, there's plenty here to inform and engage.

AI-powered Virtual Assistants

Artificial Intelligence (AI) has found its way into our everyday lives, often without us even realizing it. A significant part of this integration is through AI-powered virtual assistants like Siri, Alexa, and Google Assistant. These virtual companions have become essential tools for managing daily tasks, from setting reminders to controlling smart devices in our homes. Let's look at how they streamline these activities and the benefits they bring, ultimately making our lives more convenient and efficient.

Imagine it's the beginning of a busy day. You can simply ask your virtual assistant to remind you of meetings or to-dos. This feature takes the hassle out of keeping track of everything on your plate. Virtual assistants are programmed to understand natural language, which means you don't have to remember specific commands. Instead, you can speak casually as if conversing with a friend, and they'll grasp the task at hand. Besides reminders, these digital helpers can control various smart devices like lights, thermostats, and locks, adding a layer of convenience that was once non-existent.

The evolution of voice recognition technology has significantly contributed to the seamless operation of these assistants. Early versions often struggled with accuracy, but advancements have made them incredibly reliable. You don't need to touch your phone or device —just speak your command, and it will be executed. This hands-free interaction is handy when driving, cooking, or multitasking; situations where your hands might be preoccupied and your focus required elsewhere. The power of voice recognition doesn't just end at obeying commands; it improves user experience by learning voices over time and adapting to individual speech patterns and accents, thus enhancing communication efficacy.

Integration plays a crucial role in enriching the abilities of virtual assistants. They aren't just standalone features; their real magic happens when they're linked with other apps and services. Picture planning a day: you could ask your assistant about the weather, schedule appointments, or get traffic updates—all consolidated in one place. By acting as a hub, these assistants keep your information organized and accessible, whether you're checking emails, streaming music, or navigating to an unknown destination. This integration is not just limited to basic apps; it also includes third-party services, which expand what these assistants can achieve.

While enjoying these conveniences, it's crucial to discuss privacy concerns associated with virtual assistants, especially since they handle personal information. It's common knowledge that they listen carefully to our commands, but many might not know how their data is managed. Data collected by virtual assistants isn't stored endlessly. Instead, it's often used to improve service quality and customize user preferences. However, understanding data handling processes is key to ensuring comfort levels with these technologies. Being informed about privacy settings, such as managing voice recordings and knowing what information is shared with third parties, strengthens user confidence. Many virtual assistant platforms offer ways to review and delete interactions, allowing users to maintain control over their personal data.

To maximize privacy and security while using virtual assistants, some guidelines should be considered. First, regularly updating privacy settings ensures that you're aware of and can take advantage of new security features. Additionally, it's wise to review the permissions granted to other applications and revoke any unnecessary access. Staying informed about your device's security policies and best practices will mitigate potential risks, creating a safer environment for utilizing these helpful tools.

Smart Home Devices and AI

Smart home devices, powered by artificial intelligence (AI), are changing the way we interact with our living environments. These advancements aren't just about the wow factor of technology, but about creating a home that's more responsive and efficient. By learning from our daily routines, AI-driven automation has proven to significantly enhance the efficiency and comfort of our homes.

One of the primary ways smart devices are making an impact is through automation, responding to user patterns to help save energy. Imagine your thermostat automatically adjusting based on your behavior—cooling your house when you're typically at home and warming it up just before you arrive. This is no longer science fiction but a reality for many households. By learning when and how frequently lights, heating, and appliances are used, these systems can minimize waste, reduce bills, and lessen our carbon footprint without us having to lift a finger.

Furthermore, AI doesn't just stop at saving energy; it's also about personalizing the home atmosphere. Today's smart systems can adapt to individual preferences through machine learning algorithms. For example, lighting that adjusts its brightness or color temperature throughout the day can mimic natural light cycles, helping to improve mood and productivity. Meanwhile, smart speakers might play your favorite music as you enter a room or suggest podcasts based on your listening habits. These tailored experiences make home life not only more efficient but also uniquely comfortable and enjoyable.

Safety at home is another critical area where AI has made significant advances. AI-enhanced security cameras have become a staple in many modern homes. Unlike traditional surveillance, these cameras don't simply record footage—they analyze it in real time. They can distinguish between familiar faces, pets, and potential intruders, sending instant alerts to homeowners if something unusual occurs. This proactive approach ensures prompt action can be taken, providing peace of mind whether you're inside the house or halfway across the world.

At the heart of all these innovations is the concept of interoperability. Devices that can communicate seamlessly create a smart home ecosystem where everything works together in harmony. Consider a scenario where your alarm clock triggers your coffee maker, or your smoke detector communicates with your smart locks to ensure all doors unlock during an emergency. This interconnectedness simplifies control, allowing centralized management through a single app or voice command, bringing together various aspects of home life in a unified front.

The beauty of this integrated system lies in its simplicity and ease of use, particularly appealing to those who may find technology daunting. With user-friendly interfaces and intuitive designs, smart home technologies are accessible, ensuring that even those hesitant about technological implications can engage with and benefit from them. For those curious or skeptical about AI's role in everyday life, the incremental enhancements seen in smart homes provide persuasive evidence of its tangible advantages.

As the landscape of smart home technology continues to evolve, the possibilities seem endless. By focusing on user-specific data and habits, AI crafts a personalized experience that grows increasingly intelligent over time. It's not just about connecting devices, but about creating intelligent ecosystems that adjust to personal lifestyles.

For skeptics and tech enthusiasts alike, the progressive integration of AI in our homes presents an intriguing glimpse into the future. While there are concerns about privacy and data security, measures are continually advancing to address these challenges, ensuring that the benefits of a smarter home outweigh potential risks. As conversations around ethical AI usage grow, these discussions will undoubtedly shape how smart home technologies are developed and implemented moving forward.

Personalized Recommendations and AI

AI has become an integral part of our daily routines, often enhancing our experiences without us even realizing it. One area where AI truly shines is in delivering personalized recommendations that cater to our unique preferences and needs. These recommendations are not just about convenience; they significantly boost our engagement and satisfaction across various fields like entertainment and shopping.

Let's start with entertainment. Streaming services such as Netflix have mastered the art of content personalization through AI algorithms. When you log into your account, notice how the platform greets you with a selection of movies and shows that seem perfectly suited to your taste. This isn't mere coincidence; it's the result of complex algorithms analyzing your viewing habits—what you've watched, what you skipped, and even how long you watched certain content. By processing this data, Netflix can predict what you might enjoy next, helping you find new favorites with minimal effort on your part. This type of curation not only increases viewer satisfaction but also keeps users engaged with the platform longer, demonstrating AI's powerful role in shaping our entertainment experiences.

In the realm of e-commerce, personalized recommendations have revolutionized how we shop online. Platforms like Amazon use AI to sift through mountains of data related to your shopping behaviors, past purchases, and browsing history. With this information, they create a personalized shopping experience tailored specifically for you. The beauty of these AI-driven suggestions lies in their ability to introduce you to products you might never have discovered otherwise, fostering a deeper relationship between you and the retailer. This curated approach is not just about boosting sales; it enhances customer satisfaction by making shopping less about searching and more about exploring.

Dynamic pricing models represent another fascinating application of AI in personalizing user experiences. These models analyze a wide array of factors, including market trends, consumer demand, and even individual purchasing behaviors, to offer prices that are tailor-made for specific customers at specific times. For instance, airlines and hotel websites often adjust their prices based on when you're booking and what kind of device you're using. While some view dynamic pricing as controversial, the underlying AI technology aims to strike a balance between maximizing profits and providing deals that could encourage purchase decisions, thereby influencing how we perceive value in shopping.

Finally, social media platforms utilize AI to personalize content curation, ensuring that users see posts most relevant to them. Ever wondered why your social media feed seems to know exactly what you'd like to see or read? AI algorithms work tirelessly behind the scenes, studying your interactions—likes, shares, comments—and then tailoring your feed accordingly. This helps maintain user engagement by presenting content that resonates on a personal level. While there are ongoing discussions about the potential impacts of such personalization—including concerns over echo chambers—the intention is to enhance user experiences by focusing on content that matters most to each individual.

AI in E-commerce: Enhancing Shopping Experiences

Imagine walking into a store where you can try on clothes without even being there. Sounds futuristic, right? Well, that's exactly what AI-powered virtual fitting rooms are bringing to the online shopping experience. These innovative platforms use augmented reality and machine learning algorithms to let customers visualize how clothes will look and fit on their bodies. With just a few clicks, shoppers can explore different sizes, colors, and styles without any commitment. This not only boosts customer confidence but also significantly reduces the number of returns, which has always been a logistical headache for retailers. As customers feel more assured in their purchases, retailers gain by managing inventory more efficiently and minimizing restocking costs.

Imagine you're shopping late at night, needing an answer to a quick question about a product. Instead of waiting until morning for a response from customer service, AI-driven chatbots are here to help 24/7. These virtual assistants are designed to handle inquiries, process orders, and sometimes even provide personalized recommendations based on previous purchases. By offering round-the-clock support, these chatbots improve user satisfaction by addressing concerns immediately, which builds brand loyalty. When customers know they can rely on a retailer for instant support, they're more likely to return, turning casual browsers into dedicated buyers.

In the fast-paced world of retail, staying ahead of consumer demands is key. That's where predictive analytics come into play. Retailers are harnessing the power of AI to forecast market trends and anticipate what products will be popular. By analyzing vast amounts of data, including past sales trends, seasonality, and emerging consumer preferences, AI helps retailers make informed decisions about stock levels and product assortment. This means shelves are stocked with items customers are eager to buy, thus reducing overstock and minimizing waste. Retailers who utilize these insights can respond swiftly to changes, ensuring they keep pace with market dynamics.

We've all experienced the frustration of lengthy checkout processes, which can lead to abandoned carts. AI is streamlining this crucial step, transforming how transactions are completed. From one-click purchasing options to automated billing, AI technologies work behind the scenes to simplify and speed up the checkout process. Facial recognition or fingerprint scanning can even replace traditional payment methods, making transactions feel effortless and secure. By removing friction from the final step of online shopping, sales conversions are likely to increase, benefitting both consumers who enjoy seamless experiences and retailers who see reduced cart abandonment rates.

AI in Social Media Platforms

In our everyday lives, social media plays a significant role, and AI has become an integral part of how these platforms function. One major area where AI has made substantial contributions is in content moderation. Platforms like Facebook, Twitter, and Instagram rely on AI systems to help keep their environments safe for users. By using advanced algorithms, AI can rapidly scan and identify inappropriate or harmful content, which would be impossible for human moderators to manage at scale. These systems help remove posts that violate community guidelines, ensuring users have a safer experience online. This automated process not only speeds up moderation but also builds trust between the platform and its users, as they can see efforts being made to protect their online environment.

As we continue to scroll through our social media feeds, many might not realize that AI is curating the content we see. Algorithmically curated feeds are tailored specifically to each user, designed to show content that resonates with individual preferences and interests. For example, if you often like and comment on certain types of posts, the AI will learn from those interactions and prioritize similar content for your feed. This keeps you engaged, making it more likely for you to spend increased time on the platform. It's a strategy that benefits both users, by delivering relevant content, and social media companies, by maintaining high engagement rates. However, it's essential to remain mindful of the potential echo chamber effect, where we only see content that aligns with our current interests, potentially limiting exposure to diverse viewpoints.

AI has also streamlined the process of identifying influencers within specific niches. Social media influencers have become vital players in marketing strategies, thanks to their ability to engage vast audiences and shape consumer perceptions. AI tools can analyze vast amounts of data to spot rising stars within various communities, based on metrics such as follower growth, engagement rates, and audience demographics. Brands can then reach out to these influencers to collaborate on campaigns, knowing they speak directly to their target market. This refined marketing approach not only enhances brand visibility but also enriches user experiences by promoting products and services that align well with user interests.

Moreover, sentiment analysis tools powered by AI have allowed brands to understand public sentiment on social media better. These tools analyze text-based posts, comments, and reviews to determine the general feelings people have towards a topic, product, or brand. Businesses use this information to fine-tune their marketing campaigns, ensuring they resonate with their intended audience. By gauging whether the overall sentiment is positive, negative, or neutral, companies can adapt their strategies accordingly, adjusting messaging or addressing concerns promptly. This feedback loop, facilitated by AI, helps brands stay attuned to consumer needs and expectations, leading to more effective and responsive marketing efforts.

Concluding Thoughts

As we've explored, AI is becoming a part of our lives in ways we might not even notice. From getting reminders from virtual assistants to adjusting our home lights and thermostats, AI is here to make daily tasks easier and more personalized. It's like having an extra set of hands that remembers your preferences—it grows smarter over time to fit perfectly into your routine. While there's plenty to celebrate about these conveniences, it's also important to keep an eye on privacy concerns. Being aware of how data is used and actively managing settings helps us enjoy these benefits while staying secure.

The magic of AI doesn't stop at helping with chores; it also makes our shopping and entertainment experiences richer and more tailored to what we enjoy. Whether it's Netflix suggesting the next show you'll love or smart devices making sure your home is energy efficient, AI is quietly working to improve our world. But for all the excitement, understanding both the possibilities and risks is key. The conversation around AI's role in our lives is just getting started, and keeping it open and informed will help us navigate this tech-driven landscape confidently.

Chapter 5

Transforming Industries with AI

T ransforming industries with AI is reshaping how we understand and interact with the world around us. Whether it's predicting patient outcomes in healthcare or automating complex tasks in manufacturing, AI's influence is both profound and pervasive. Imagine a world where your doctor has the tools to diagnose illnesses faster than ever before or where financial transactions are seamlessly secured from fraud. At the heart of this transformation is AI's capacity to enhance efficiency, boost innovation, and tailor experiences across a multitude of domains. The shift isn't just about substituting human expertise but augmenting it to unlock new potentials. As AI continues to evolve, its role in shaping sectors like healthcare, finance, and education becomes increasingly evident, promising improvements that not only streamline operations but also enrich daily lives.

In this chapter, we explore how AI is causing waves of change across various industries, making them more innovative, efficient, and personalized. From revolutionizing healthcare with predictive analytics and advanced diagnostics to transforming finance through automated trading and fraud detection, AI's footprint is undeniably significant. We delve into the ways AI enhances manufacturing processes, ensuring precision while reducing waste, and examine its impact on transportation, where autonomous systems and intelligent traffic management redefine mobility. Additionally, we discuss AI's revolutionary contributions to education, from personalizing learning experiences to easing administrative workloads. By highlighting these diverse applications, the chapter sheds light on the vast potential AI holds for reshaping traditional practices and ushering in a future of enhanced possibilities. Through these explorations, we aim to foster an understanding of AI's transformative capabilities and provoke thoughtful discussions on its integration and ethical implications in our everyday lives.

Healthcare Advancements through AI

Artificial Intelligence (AI) is making waves across various industries, and healthcare is no exception. It's transforming the way we diagnose, treat, and prevent illnesses. One significant change AI brings is improving the accuracy of medical diagnostics. Using advanced pattern recognition, AI software can sift through vast amounts of data to pick out patterns that even the most experienced doctors might miss. For example, in radiology, AI systems have been developed to analyze images such as X-rays, MRIs, and CT scans more rapidly and, in some cases, more accurately than human radiologists. This doesn't mean that doctors are being replaced; instead, AI is being used as a tool that augments their expertise, allowing for faster and potentially more accurate diagnoses.

Another area where AI is revolutionizing healthcare is predictive analytics. By analyzing historical data from millions of patients, AI tools can forecast patient outcomes and suggest preventive measures. These tools help healthcare providers plan better interventions, reducing complications and overall costs. For instance, hospitals use predictive analytics to identify patients at high risk for readmission. With this information, they can ensure these patients receive appropriate follow-up care, ultimately lowering readmission rates and associated costs. It's a win-win situation for both healthcare systems striving for efficiency and patients seeking cost-effective care.

Drug discovery is yet another frontier where AI's influence is palpable. The development of new medications is traditionally a slow, costly process with many stages, often taking years to bring a new drug to market. AI expedites this process by simulating biological processes and predicting how different compounds will interact with targets in the body. Through machine learning algorithms, AI can quickly point researchers toward the most promising compounds, significantly speeding up the initial phases of drug discovery. A notable example is the recent COVID-19 pandemic, where AI played a crucial role in identifying candidate molecules for antiviral therapies, reducing the time needed by traditional methods.

Telemedicine, too, is benefiting immensely from AI innovations. As the global pandemic necessitated remote consultations, AI-driven virtual health assistants and personalized health reminders became more prevalent. These virtual assistants can perform various tasks, such as setting appointment reminders, providing medication alerts, or offering preliminary advice before a doctor consultation. Moreover, AI-powered chatbots now handle routine queries, helping reduce the workload on healthcare professionals and allowing them to focus more on complex cases. These tools not only make healthcare more accessible but also cater to the growing demand for personalization and convenience among patients.

This wave of innovation, driven by AI, does come with its set of challenges and ethical considerations. While AI holds enormous potential to improve healthcare delivery and outcomes, it's essential to address concerns about data privacy, security, and the need for robust regulatory frameworks. New technologies must prioritize patient confidentiality and ensure that AI systems are transparent and fair. In addition, as AI systems begin to play a more prominent role in decision-making, healthcare professionals must receive adequate training to effectively integrate these tools into their practices without undermining their own clinical judgment.

Yet, despite these challenges, one thing is clear: AI is poised to revolutionize healthcare in unprecedented ways. While the technology is still evolving, it promises a future where healthcare is more efficient, accurate, and personalized than ever before. Patients will benefit from faster diagnostics, customized treatment plans, and, overall, a higher quality of care. Meanwhile, healthcare providers will be equipped with tools that enhance their capabilities and allow them to focus on the human touch that's so critical in patient care.

AI in Finance: Automation and Analysis

When we think about the world of finance, it's fascinating to see how artificial intelligence (AI) has woven itself into its very fabric, reshaping processes and strategies in ways that were once unimaginable. Take trading, for instance. Gone are the days when stock market decisions relied solely on gut instinct or basic data analysis. Now, AI-driven algorithms have transformed trading by optimizing strategies through the meticulous analysis of real-time financial data.

These algorithms sift through vast amounts of information, identifying patterns and trends with precision far beyond human capability. They allow traders to make split-second decisions based on the latest market conditions, ensuring they stay ahead of the curve. Whether it's predicting a stock's movement or spotting lucrative investment opportunities, AI provides the edge needed to thrive in today's volatile markets.

Fraud detection is another area where AI shines brightly. Financial institutions constantly battle against fraudulent activities that can result in significant losses. Traditional methods of fraud detection often lag behind, giving perpetrators the upper hand. However, AI has revolutionized these systems, enabling the real-time identification of suspicious activities. By analyzing transaction patterns and user behaviors, AI-powered systems can flag anomalies that may indicate fraud. This proactive approach not only saves money but also protects consumer trust, which is vital in the financial industry.

Let's not overlook personal finance management apps, which have become indispensable tools for many individuals. Imagine receiving personalized financial advice tailored specifically to your spending habits. That's precisely what AI offers. These apps analyze your income, expenses, and even minor spending nuances to provide insights that help you manage your finances better. Whether it's suggesting a new budget plan, warning about overspending, or recommending suitable investment options, AI turns your smartphone into a financial advisor in your pocket.

Risk management, a cornerstone of any solid financial strategy, has seen remarkable improvements through AI's predictive analytics capabilities. In the complex world of finance, assessing market conditions accurately is crucial. AI models can predict shifts in economic indicators or market trends, allowing financial professionals to devise strategies that mitigate risks effectively. This kind of foresight helps institutions maintain stability even when external events threaten to disrupt their operations.

Imagine, for example, a sudden geopolitical event that could potentially affect global markets. Thanks to AI, risk managers can simulate various scenarios and evaluate their potential impacts, enabling them to prepare contingency plans well in advance. As a result, companies can navigate turbulent times with confidence, safeguarding their assets and securing long-term growth.

Revolutionizing Transportation with AI

In today's fast-paced world, technology is reshaping industries in unprecedented ways. One of the most noticeable changes is happening within the transportation sector, largely driven by advancements in Artificial Intelligence (AI). Let's dive into how AI is transforming this essential aspect of our everyday lives.

Autonomous vehicles are one of the most talked-about applications of AI in transportation. These self-driving cars use complex algorithms to navigate roads, interpret signals, and detect objects around them. Essentially, AI allows these vehicles to "see" their surroundings and make decisions based on that information. This capability substantially reduces human error, which is a leading cause of accidents on the road. With fewer accidents, we can expect not only safer roads but also reduced congestion, as these vehicles communicate with each other to optimize traffic flow more efficiently than humans ever could. While there's still some way to go before autonomous vehicles dominate the roads, their potential for revolutionizing transportation is immense.

Another substantial contribution of AI to transportation is through traffic management systems. AI-driven traffic lights and control systems adapt in real-time to changing conditions. Imagine a city where traffic lights adjust themselves automatically based on the current flow of vehicles, reducing bottlenecks and minimizing delays. These intelligent systems can also analyze data from various sources, such as cameras and sensors, to predict and prevent congestion before it even occurs. By optimizing traffic flow, these systems enhance commuter experiences and decrease travel times significantly.

Logistics is another area seeing profound improvements due to AI. In the past, companies relied heavily on manual calculations and somewhat static systems to plan routes and manage inventory. Today, AI has turned logistics into a highly dynamic and efficient process. Algorithms now analyze vast amounts of data — including weather forecasts, traffic patterns, and delivery windows — to find the most efficient routes for deliveries. This optimization not only saves time and fuel costs but also ensures timely deliveries, improving customer satisfaction. Moreover, AI helps manage inventory more effectively by predicting demand and adjusting stock levels accordingly, greatly reducing waste and boosting profitability.

When it comes to ride-sharing services, AI's influence is equally significant. Companies like Uber and Lyft utilize AI to perfect dynamic pricing models that balance supply and demand. This ensures that prices remain competitive while drivers have an incentive to work during peak hours. Additionally, AI enhances the efficiency of matching passengers with drivers. By analyzing data on location, traffic, and driver availability, these services can assign rides quickly and accurately, reducing wait times for everyone involved. The overall result is a smoother, more reliable experience for both drivers and riders.

Each of these areas demonstrates how AI is gradually weaving itself into the fabric of transportation, making it smarter and more effective. However, it's important to acknowledge that these advancements come with considerations about privacy, security, and job displacement. As we embrace these technologies, ongoing discussions and evaluations will be necessary to address concerns and ensure that everyone benefits.

AI's Role in Manufacturing Processes

Artificial Intelligence (AI) is making waves across industries, but one place it's truly transforming is manufacturing. Picture this: factories running smoother than ever, with less waste and more productivity. That's the magic of AI at work! Let's dive into how AI is boosting productivity and cutting down on waste.

To start, consider predictive maintenance. It used to be that machines would break down unexpectedly, leaving production lines at a standstill. With AI, manufacturers can predict when equipment might fail and fix issues before they cause downtime. Sensors collect data from machines, and AI analyzes this information to foresee problems. Imagine being able to replace a part just before it breaks—not only does this prevent unexpected halts, but it also extends the machinery's lifespan. This means fewer replacements and repairs, saving both time and resources. It's like having an early warning system that's right on target, keeping everything running smoothly.

Next up is quality control—which has traditionally been labor-intensive and prone to human error. Now, AI steps in with machine vision technology. This allows for real-time inspection of products during manufacturing. AI systems scrutinize items with precision far beyond human capabilities, spotting even minuscule defects or deviations from the standard. For instance, in the electronics industry, where components are incredibly small and intricacies matter, AI ensures each piece meets quality standards. What does this mean for manufacturers? Higher-quality products rolling off the line with less waste due to faulty items being caught early on. This not only boosts quality but assures customers they're getting top-notch products every time.

The supply chain is another area seeing incredible changes thanks to AI. Traditionally, predicting demand was a mix of guesswork and historical trend analysis, which isn't always accurate and often leads to surplus stock or shortages. AI revolutionizes this by using advanced algorithms to forecast demand more precisely. It considers a variety of factors, including market trends and consumer behavior, adjusting supplies accordingly. This results in a finely-tuned balance where neither excess inventory nor scarcity becomes an issue. The outcome? Reduced waste and optimized resources leading to both cost savings and increased customer satisfaction. When the right amount of product is produced and delivered at the right time, everyone wins.

We can't talk about manufacturing without mentioning robotics and automation. These technologies have been around, but AI takes them to a whole new level. AI-powered robots are now capable of learning tasks, adapting to new processes, and working alongside humans more efficiently than ever. They handle repetitive, mundane jobs quickly and accurately, freeing up human workers for more complex tasks that require creativity and decision-making. In high-risk environments or tasks involving dangerous materials, AI-powered automation enhances safety. By taking over these perilous duties, it helps reduce workplace accidents—making factories not just more productive, but safer too.

Think about the collaborative robots—or "cobots"—that are designed to work in tandem with human colleagues. AI enables them to understand and anticipate human actions, creating a seamless partnership between man and machine. This collaboration increases efficiency as tasks can be completed faster and with fewer errors. Moreover, cobots are flexible; they can be reprogrammed for different tasks as needed, making them highly adaptable to changing demands or new production lines. This versatility is key in today's fast-paced, ever-evolving manufacturing landscape.

Overall, AI's role in manufacturing is transformative. It's not just about doing things faster, although that's a big part of it. It's about doing them smarter, with greater precision, and with a focus on sustainability. Reducing waste isn't just about cutting costs—it's important for environmental reasons as well. AI helps achieve greener practices by optimizing resource use, reducing raw material wastage, and enhancing energy efficiency through improved process controls.

For those a bit skeptical about embracing these technologies, it's essential to consider the potential benefits. AI doesn't just replace human roles; it enhances them and creates opportunities for more fulfilling work. As AI continues to evolve, so will its applications in manufacturing, promising even greater advances in productivity and sustainability. Embracing AI is not just about keeping up with trends— it's about paving the way for a future where industries can thrive while conserving resources for the planet.

Education and Personalized Learning with AI

In the evolving landscape of education, AI plays a pivotal role in redefining how learning is personalized and how educational advancements are achieved. At the forefront of this transformation are adaptive learning platforms, which harness the power of AI to customize the learning experience for each student. Unlike traditional methods where every student receives the same content, adaptive learning systems evaluate individual performance and learning styles to tailor educational resources accordingly. Imagine a student struggling with algebra; the platform automatically senses the challenge and adjusts the pace or introduces supplementary resources to help the learner grasp concepts more effectively. This personalized learning approach not only enhances comprehension but also boosts confidence by allowing students to progress at their own speed.

Shifting focus from learning to logistics, AI significantly lightens the administrative burden on educators. Traditionally time-consuming tasks like grading can now be automated through AI algorithms, enabling teachers to dedicate more time to what truly matters—teaching and mentoring students. Automated grading systems quickly assess assignments, providing instant feedback to students while ensuring consistency and objectivity. This automation doesn't just save time; it opens doors for educators to engage in creative lesson planning and student interaction, fostering a more dynamic and engaged classroom environment.

Another remarkable application of AI in education is through virtual tutors, which offer students round-the-clock academic support. These intelligent systems are designed to provide homework assistance and study guidance whenever needed. Picture a high school student stuck on a late-night chemistry problem; an AI-driven tutor can step in immediately, offering explanations, breaking down complex ideas, and helping the student work through challenges independently. This accessibility empowers students to learn outside traditional school hours, encouraging self-paced and self-motivated learning experiences that align with modern lifestyles.

Furthermore, AI provides invaluable data-driven insights that can transform how curricula are designed and implemented. By analyzing vast amounts of educational data, AI systems can identify trends and patterns in student performance. For instance, if a significant number of students consistently encounter difficulties with a particular topic, AI can flag this issue, prompting educators to revisit and perhaps revise their teaching strategies for that subject area. These insights enable a proactive rather than reactive approach to curriculum development, ensuring that educational content remains relevant, challenging, and effective.

Embracing AI in education requires acknowledging both its capabilities and limitations. While these technologies offer unprecedented efficiencies and enhancements, they also prompt discussions about privacy, data security, and the ethics of relying heavily on machines in educational settings. As we integrate AI solutions, it's crucial to balance technological advancement with human oversight, ensuring that AI acts as an adjunct to, rather than a replacement for, skilled educators. Teachers bring empathy, creativity, and adaptability—qualities that machines cannot replicate.

The ongoing dialogue about AI's role in education fosters a more informed and nuanced understanding of both its potential and pitfalls. For instance, concerns about over-reliance on technology or the digital divide, where access to these advanced tools might be limited, necessitate thoughtful consideration and strategic approaches to implementation. Ensuring equitable access to AI-enhanced learning tools is vital to prevent widening gaps between students in different socioeconomic settings.

Final Thoughts

Throughout this chapter, we've taken a closer look at how AI is transforming different sectors, from healthcare to education, by boosting innovation, efficiency, and personalization. In healthcare, for example, AI helps doctors diagnose illnesses faster and more accurately, predicts patient outcomes, and even speeds up drug discovery. This means better care for patients and more efficient systems all around. In finance, AI enhances trading strategies, detects fraud in real-time, and offers personalized financial advice, making financial services smarter and safer. As we shift gears to transportation, AI's role in developing self-driving cars and improving traffic flow reveals its potential to make our commutes safer and more efficient.

Moving on, AI's influence extends into manufacturing where it optimizes processes like predictive maintenance and quality control, helping factories run smoother and waste less. And in education, it's all about personalizing learning and easing teachers' workloads through adaptive platforms and virtual tutors. While each sector encounters unique challenges with AI, such as privacy concerns or job displacement, the benefits highlight AI's ability to revolutionize industries by making everyday tasks more manageable. Importantly, embracing these changes presents opportunities not just for professionals curious about AI's impact on their fields but also for skeptics and lifelong learners aiming to understand and engage with technology's evolving landscape.

Chapter 6

Understanding AI's Benefits

U nderstanding AI's benefits is like opening up a new world of possibilities. It's not just about robots or high-tech gadgets; it's about reshaping our everyday lives in ways we might not even realize. From how businesses operate to simplifying the mundane tasks in our daily routines, AI quietly but effectively enhances the way we live and work. Imagine your day-to-day life with a bit of extra help from technology that's smart enough to manage repetitive tasks, freeing you up to focus on what truly matters. It's this subtle blend of efficiency and innovation where AI makes its mark, inviting us to consider how much better off we can be when technology and human effort come together.

In this chapter, we'll delve into some of the most exciting aspects of AI that are making waves today. Get ready to explore how AI boosts efficiency, reduces errors, and cuts costs across various sectors, showing us why it's such a hot topic right now. We'll also touch upon the impact of data analytics and how AI drives innovation forward, painting a picture of what the future could look like. Whether you're curious, skeptical, or just eager to learn more, there's something here for everyone as we navigate the ins and outs of AI's positive contributions to society. So, buckle up as we embark on this journey to understand and appreciate the multifaceted advantages AI brings to the table.

Efficiency Improvement in Operations

Artificial intelligence, or AI for short, is playing a transformative role in how we manage our everyday work tasks, and one of the most significant areas where it shines is in automating routine activities. Imagine having to spend hours sorting through emails, scheduling meetings, or handling basic customer inquiries. These repetitive tasks can be mind-numbing and eat away at valuable time that could be better spent on more strategic initiatives. AI changes the game here by taking over such mundane tasks, allowing human resources to engage in activities that require creative thinking and problem-solving skills — things machines can't replicate.

Consider a customer support center. Instead of employees answering basic questions all day long, AI-powered chatbots can handle these queries with precision and speed, freeing up staff to tackle more complex issues or develop strategies for improving customer satisfaction. This shift not only enhances productivity but also boosts employee morale, as workers find themselves engaged in more fulfilling roles.

Moving into another realm, AI's impact on supply chain optimization is nothing short of revolutionary. Managing logistics and inventory has traditionally been a headache for businesses, with constant juggling required to prevent delays and ensure smooth operations. Here, AI platforms analyze data from various points in the supply chain to predict demand, optimize delivery routes, and manage stock levels more efficiently. By doing so, companies can avoid costly delays and shortages, keeping their customers happy and their products flowing smoothly.

For example, consider retail giants like Amazon. They use AI to forecast which products will be in demand, allowing them to stock up accordingly and deliver orders promptly. This technology isn't limited to large corporations — small businesses can also reap the benefits by utilizing AI tools tailored to their needs. As a result, whether it's a local boutique or a multinational corporation, leveraging AI for supply chain management leads to streamlined operations and improved service delivery.

Resource allocation is another critical area where AI insights make a noticeable difference. In any organization, understanding where to deploy resources effectively can mean the difference between success and overspending. AI helps in making these decisions by providing detailed analysis of data patterns and trends. This analysis aids in identifying areas that need attention and those that are performing well, allowing managers to allocate budgets and manpower efficiently.

Imagine a healthcare facility using AI to determine peak times for patient visits. With this information, they can ensure staff is available when needed most, reducing wait times and improving patient care. Similarly, in manufacturing, AI might suggest reallocating resources from over-performing units to underperforming ones to maintain balance and efficiency. The outcome is a more synchronized operation that cuts down unnecessary expenditures while maximizing returns on investment.

One of the more promising applications of AI lies in optimizing energy consumption. We live in a world increasingly focused on sustainability, and AI offers innovative solutions for reducing energy use while enhancing operational resilience. Smart grids, powered by AI, allow for real-time monitoring and management of energy usage across multiple locations. This capability results in lower energy costs and reduced carbon footprints, contributing positively to environmental goals.

Take, for example, smart thermostats that learn user habits over time. They adjust heating and cooling based on occupancy patterns, ensuring that energy is used only when necessary. Large office buildings employ similar technologies to manage lighting, HVAC systems, and more, significantly reducing energy waste. This kind of intelligent energy management makes facilities more sustainable and cost-effective, proving beneficial both economically and ecologically.

AI's Potential to Reduce Human Error

Artificial intelligence (AI) is transforming how we interact with and utilize technology, offering significant advantages in minimizing errors often associated with human judgment and abilities. One of the most compelling benefits lies in AI's precision in data analysis. Traditionally, manual data processing involves a considerable risk of miscalculations due to human error, whether from fatigue or oversight. AI algorithms, however, have the capability to sift through massive datasets with unparalleled accuracy. This precision allows for more informed decision-making and insights that might otherwise be missed.

Take, for instance, the financial sector. Here, even minor errors can lead to substantial financial losses. AI provides a robust solution by employing machine learning models that analyze past and present trends to predict future occurrences. This sort of predictive analytics not only mitigates risk but also offers firms a reliable foundation to build their strategies on. Fraud detection has seen remarkable improvements thanks to AI's capabilities. Unlike traditional methods that might fail to detect anomalies in a timely fashion, AI systems continuously learn and adapt, identifying fraudulent activities with greater speed and reliability. By scanning transaction histories and user profiles, these systems spot unusual patterns that might indicate fraud, thereby safeguarding assets and maintaining trust.

Quality assurance in manufacturing has similarly benefited from AI advancements. Human eyes scrutinizing production lines are prone to fatigue, potentially overlooking defects that could compromise product quality. Instead, AI-driven systems use computer vision technologies to monitor production processes in real-time. These smart systems can identify defects far more quickly and consistently than human inspectors, ensuring that the quality of goods produced meets the desired standards. Consequently, manufacturers witness a reduction in waste, improved efficiency, and an increase in customer satisfaction as defective products are intercepted before reaching the market.

The medical field is another area where AI's error-reducing capabilities shine brightly. Diagnostic accuracy is crucial because it directly affects patient outcomes. AI applications in medical imaging, such as analyzing X-rays, MRIs, and CT scans, provide physicians with highly accurate assessments by identifying patterns that may not be readily apparent to the human eye. Such tools enhance a doctor's ability to diagnose diseases at earlier stages, ultimately leading to better patient prognosis. Moreover, AI in pathology helps process large volumes of patient data swiftly, allowing for faster identification of diseases based on historical data trends and genetic information. This integration ensures that diagnostic procedures are not only more efficient but also less prone to the subjective biases that can sometimes influence human judgment.

In financial analysis, beyond fraud detection, AI plays a crucial role in risk assessment. Financial markets are highly dynamic, with innumerable variables influencing outcomes. Human analysts might struggle to keep pace with this complexity, occasionally resulting in errors that affect investment decisions. AI, on the other hand, processes vast amounts of market data practically in real time, assessing risks based on a multitude of factors, from economic indicators to geopolitical events. It identifies trends and presents forecasts with a depth and speed unattainable by human means, enabling investors to make decisions with greater confidence and precision.

Furthermore, in customer service sectors, AI minimizes errors by automating responses and general inquiries, removing the inconsistencies in manual customer interactions. AI-powered chatbots can handle multiple queries simultaneously without sacrificing response quality. They learn from each interaction, gradually improving at delivering personalized and accurate replies. This not only elevates customer satisfaction by reducing wait times but also allows human representatives to focus on more complex issues that require nuanced understanding.

While AI's capacity to reduce errors is impressive, it's essential to acknowledge its limitations. AI systems must be carefully designed and maintained, as biases and inaccuracies can still emerge if the underlying data is flawed. However, with ongoing advancements in AI research and implementation, there is a continuous push to refine these systems, ensuring they complement human effort while minimizing potential downsides.

Cost Reduction in Business Processes

Implementing AI in business operations offers a wealth of benefits, particularly when it comes to cost savings. One of the most notable advantages is AI's ability to identify inefficiencies and streamline operations, effectively reducing costs even in the face of market fluctuations. By analyzing vast amounts of data, AI can spot patterns and optimize processes that might not be immediately apparent to human analysts. For instance, AI systems can monitor energy usage within a facility, providing actionable insights to minimize waste and reduce utility costs.

Furthermore, integrating predictive maintenance in manufacturing is another area where AI can significantly cut costs. Traditionally, equipment maintenance schedules have been based on estimated timelines or after a breakdown occurs, leading to unplanned downtimes and costly repairs. Predictive maintenance, facilitated by AI, uses data collected from various sensors to predict when a machine is likely to fail. This approach ensures maintenance is performed only when necessary, optimizing maintenance budgets and preventing unexpected production halts.

Incorporating customer support automation through AI-driven chatbots is another way businesses are cutting costs. These chatbots can handle a myriad of common customer inquiries without human intervention, freeing up customer service representatives to tackle more complex issues. As a result, businesses can operate with smaller support teams while maintaining or even enhancing customer satisfaction levels. The chatbots are available 24/7, ensuring customers receive immediate responses, which further adds to the overall positive experience.

Moreover, AI facilitates personalized training programs within companies, offering another avenue for cost reduction. Traditional training methods often require significant time and resources, involving hiring trainers, booking venues, and pulling employees away from their duties. AI-powered platforms can assess each employee's learning style and pace, tailoring training content accordingly. This personalization ensures employees learn more efficiently, saving both time and resources as they can complete training at their own pace and according to their specific needs.

AI's ability to streamline operations plays a crucial role in helping businesses navigate economic turbulence. By automating repetitive tasks and optimizing supply chains, companies can remain agile and respond quickly to changes in consumer demand or supply chain disruptions. For example, AI can help adjust inventory orders dynamically based on real-time sales data, ensuring businesses maintain optimal stock levels without overproducing or understocking.

The importance of predictive maintenance cannot be overstated. It's particularly valuable in industries like manufacturing, where machinery forms the backbone of operations. Unplanned downtime in such sectors equates to significant financial loss. By predicting potential failures, AI enables preemptive repairs, minimizing disruption. A case in point is Rolls-Royce, which employs AI to analyze engine data, allowing them to perform maintenance before failure occurs, thus reducing costs associated with unexpected repairs and grounding of aircrafts.

In customer service, AI-driven chatbots offer more than just financial savings. They also enhance the customer experience, creating loyalty and repeat business. By resolving queries rapidly, they improve customer satisfaction rates and free up human agents to provide better service on complicated issues that demand a personal touch. For businesses aiming at scaling operations while keeping expenditure in check, these chatbots are invaluable assets.

Meanwhile, the development of personalized training programs powered by AI serves as a catalyst for enhanced employee engagement and productivity. Employees receive tailored learning experiences suited to their roles and learning preferences, which improves knowledge retention. Companies like IBM use AI to create custom learning paths for employees, which helps ensure workers acquire necessary skills efficiently. This targeted approach results in employees being more competent and confident in their job roles, driving operational excellence.

Despite initial investments in AI technologies, the long-term savings and efficiency gains make it an attractive proposition for businesses across sectors. Organizations adopting AI can not only save substantial costs but also gain a competitive edge by operating more intelligently and responsively compared to those who lag behind in technological adoption. The key lies in understanding specific business challenges and strategically deploying AI solutions to address them, ensuring maximum return on investment.

Enhanced Data Analytics Capabilities

In today's fast-paced world, the ability to make quick and informed decisions can be the difference between success and failure. That's where AI's real-time data processing comes into play. Imagine a scenario where a retail business wants to optimize its stock levels based on consumer behavior. Traditionally, this would require manual tracking and extensive analysis of sales patterns over time—a time-consuming endeavor. However, with AI, these businesses can process vast amounts of data almost instantaneously, providing them with immediate insights. This enables them to adjust inventory, tailor marketing strategies, and even predict future trends with remarkable agility. The impact is clear: faster decision-making leads to more responsive and competitive operations.

But the capabilities of AI don't stop at merely speeding up processes; they delve into depths that were once inaccessible to human analysis. Let's consider complex data interpretation. It's one thing to look at numbers and charts, but it's another to uncover hidden patterns and trends within them. AI excels at this by using advanced algorithms to sift through enormous datasets, identifying connections and anomalies that might elude even the most experienced analyst. For example, in the healthcare sector, AI can analyze medical records, genetic information, and clinical trial data to uncover correlations that inform better treatment plans and outcomes. This kind of intelligent interpretation transforms raw data into actionable insights, pushing industries toward novel solutions and innovations.

Moreover, as AI becomes increasingly adept at interpreting complex data, it also helps bridge the gap between technical experts and those without specialized knowledge. One way it does this is through data visualization tools. Picture a dashboard that translates intricate metrics into intuitive and visually appealing graphs or charts. These tools present an opportunity for non-technical stakeholders, like company executives or marketing teams, to engage with data meaningfully. By seeing the bigger picture in a simplified format, these individuals can contribute to discussions and strategies they might otherwise have felt excluded from due to a lack of technical expertise. This fosters seamless collaboration across different departments, enhancing overall organizational synergy.

In addition, AI's integration capabilities bring diverse data sources together, offering a more comprehensive view of operational environments. Modern organizations often rely on multiple systems and platforms—each generating data independently. Whether it's from sales, customer service, social media, or supply chain management, these various streams can sometimes seem disjointed. AI has the power to unify them, drawing insights from disparate datasets to provide a cohesive understanding of the organization as a whole. Think about how this could revamp strategic planning sessions: with integrated data, decision-makers can see every facet of the business landscape, anticipate issues before they arise, and align their objectives more effectively.

Imagine a sprawling metropolis utilizing AI to manage its public transport system. The city collects data from traffic sensors, commuter apps, weather forecasts, and even social media chatter about public transportation experiences. Without AI, organizing this multitude of inputs would be daunting, likely resulting in fragmented and inefficient responses to congestion challenges. With AI, however, these inputs are processed collectively, enabling city planners to devise innovative solutions such as dynamic traffic signal adjustments or optimized bus routes, ultimately enhancing commuter experiences and reducing travel times.

These examples only scratch the surface of AI's potential to transform the way we interact with data. But they illustrate crucial points: AI's ability to process data in real-time equips us with immediacy in our responses, its capacity to interpret complex datasets unlocks new possibilities, visualization tools democratize data access and foster collaborative efforts, and integration paints a complete picture we couldn't achieve on our own. We are just beginning to explore AI's transformative impact on data utilization, and its promise remains vast and exciting.

For individuals in professions that require staying informed about technological advancements, understanding these aspects of AI opens doors to embracing change rather than fearing it. Skeptics might question whether relying on machines for these tasks diminishes human involvement, but the truth is that AI acts as a powerful augmenting tool. It doesn't replace the value of human intuition and creativity; instead, it amplifies our capabilities, allowing us to focus on higher-level problem-solving and strategy.

Lifelong learners and technology enthusiasts find themselves in an era ripe with opportunities to engage with AI-driven developments. With a foundational grasp of AI's benefits in data processing and interpretation, they can participate in broader conversations about its potential impacts. Embracing AI does not mean sacrificing ethical considerations or societal values. Rather, it invites us to sculpt how these technologies advance progress responsibly and inclusively. The journey involves ongoing dialogue—from harnessing AI's strengths to addressing its implications—ensuring that the road ahead is paved with understanding, innovation, and collaboration.

Innovation Acceleration via AI

AI is a game changer, especially when it comes to driving innovation across different sectors. It's like having a super-efficient assistant that helps researchers and companies achieve breakthroughs more quickly and cost-effectively. Take pharmaceuticals, for example. The process of developing new drugs used to take years, often dragging on because of the extensive research and testing involved. However, AI has sped up these R&D processes dramatically. By using sophisticated algorithms to predict outcomes and simulate drug interactions, scientists can now reduce both the time and resources needed to bring a product from concept to market. This doesn't just save money; it also means life-saving medications reach patients faster.

Similarly, in the tech world, AI plays a significant role in shortening development cycles. Companies utilize machine learning models to rapidly prototype and test solutions before they ever hit the shelves. This quick turnaround means that technological advancements happen at a breathtaking pace, keeping companies competitive in fast-moving industries. A guideline here for those in R&D: leverage AI-driven simulations and predictive analytics to identify potential pitfalls early in the development phase. Doing so can significantly cut down on trial-and-error phases, saving precious time and resources.

Shifting gears, let's talk about how AI enhances product development. In today's consumer-driven market, understanding what customers truly want can be tricky. AI comes into play by providing valuable feedback and insights. Through data analysis and machine learning, businesses can analyze consumer behavior patterns and preferences more accurately than ever. This isn't just about creating products but crafting solutions that meet specific needs, sometimes even before consumers know they have them. It's like having a crystal ball that models trends and predicts future demands.

Moreover, AI-generated feedback loops allow for constant product refinement. Imagine a scenario where a company releases a new gadget and uses AI tools to track user satisfaction in real-time. If something isn't working well, the business can tweak the product continuously until it aligns perfectly with user expectations. This dynamic approach creates a win-win situation for both companies and consumers, fostering loyalty and satisfaction through personalized experiences.

Creativity might seem like a domain uniquely human, yet AI is making significant strides here as well. Artists and musicians are collaborating with AI systems to create groundbreaking work that might never have been possible otherwise. For instance, AI can compose music or paint stunning pieces by analyzing countless existing works and generating something entirely new. These tools don't replace human creativity but complement it, offering artists fresh inspiration and pushing creative boundaries. Musicians can experiment with AI to mix new sounds or develop compositions that wow audiences and challenge traditional norms.

In photography and video production, AI helps create unique visual effects and edits that would require much more time if done manually. Combining artistic intuition with AI's analytical prowess paves the way for innovative projects that captivate and engage audiences globally. The novel advancements achieved through these collaborations underscore AI's potential in expanding the horizons of creative fields.

Let's not forget about the emergence of new business models thanks to AI's remarkable adaptability. As technology continues to evolve, traditional business practices must adapt to keep up with changing consumer behaviors and expectations. AI assists businesses in reimagining their strategies through enhanced consumer engagement and clever market positioning. By analyzing vast amounts of data, AI can unearth patterns that inform more effective marketing tactics and customer interaction strategies.

Consider a retail company using AI-driven chatbots for customer service. These bots provide instant responses, round-the-clock support, and handle simple queries efficiently. But that's just the tip of the iceberg. Through natural language processing, these chatbots learn from each interaction, improving over time and providing even better service. Businesses leveraging this technology enhance customer experience while freeing up human resources for more complex tasks.

Furthermore, AI fuels personalized marketing strategies. By tracking user habits and preferences, companies can tailor advertisements and offers to individual consumers, increasing the chances of conversion. This personalization extends to the shopping experience itself—recommendation engines powered by AI suggest products based on previous searches and purchases, delighting customers with intuitive suggestions they actually want.

Beyond just customer engagement, AI influences how companies position themselves in the market. Harnessing AI insights, businesses can launch new services that align with consumer needs or pivot swiftly to capture emerging opportunities. This agility fosters resilience and allows companies to stay one step ahead in an increasingly competitive landscape.

Summary and Reflections

As we've explored in this chapter, AI is transforming our world by enhancing efficiency, reducing errors, cutting costs, and unleashing a wave of innovation. It's paving the way for a future where mundane tasks are automated, freeing up human energy for more creative and strategic endeavors. By optimizing processes in businesses big and small, AI not only saves money but also boosts productivity and employee satisfaction. From supply chain management to resource allocation, AI is a powerful tool that helps organizations run smoother and smarter.

Moreover, AI's ability to analyze data with incredible precision minimizes human error, ensuring better decision-making across sectors. Whether it's improving diagnostic accuracy in healthcare or detecting financial fraud, AI applications are making our lives safer and more convenient. It's fascinating to see how AI can even spark creativity, offering new avenues for artists and musicians to explore. This journey into the world of AI reveals its potential to revolutionize how we live and work, inviting all of us, regardless of our technical background, to engage with these exciting advancements for a brighter tomorrow.

Chapter 7

Addressing the Ethical Concerns of AI

U nderstanding the ethical concerns of AI in our everyday lives is becoming more and more important. You've probably heard how AI is shaping everything from how we shop to how cities monitor public safety. With every click and swipe, there's a system collecting data, learning, and making decisions that affect us all. This technology isn't just about convenience or cutting-edge innovation; it dives into some pretty deep ethical waters like privacy, civil liberties, and what it means when machines start making choices that impact humans. In this chapter, we're going to unravel these complex moral puzzles. So, whether you're browsing online or walking through crowded streets under electronic eyes, there's a lot more than meets the eye.

We're diving headfirst into the core issues around AI ethics with a focus on privacy. First up, we'll chat about how AI systems gather data—lots of it—and what that means for your personal privacy. No one likes feeling watched, right? We'll also explore how AI influences surveillance and what that does to our freedoms. It's not just about prying eyes on city streets but understanding the bigger picture of who controls that data and how it's used. It's kind of like pulling back the curtain on the wizard of Oz. Plus, we'll look into concepts like the "Right to Forget," which might sound nice, but really comes with its own set of challenges in the digital world. Transparency and informed consent will be themes here, too, because knowing what's happening with your information should never be left in the dark. Lastly, we'll touch on how secure all this information is—spoiler alert: breaches happen, and they're a big deal. There's a lot at stake, so buckle up as we take a closer look at the ethical implications that come with the amazing power of AI.

Privacy Concerns in AI Applications

In today's digital age, AI is more intertwined with our lives than many might realize. However, this intertwining isn't without concerns, particularly when it comes to privacy. Let's dig a little deeper into data collection practices and their potential implications on individual privacy.

AI systems thrive on data, consuming vast quantities to function effectively. Every time you shop online or use a navigation app, data is collected. This constant gathering of information can lead to serious privacy violations if not handled properly. For example, even non-sensitive data like shopping preferences or travel routes can be pieced together to create detailed profiles about individuals. This raises questions about who has access to this data and for what purposes they are using it.

One notable concern is the rise of AI in surveillance. In recent years, numerous cities have implemented AI-driven surveillance systems to enhance public security. While these technologies can help in crime prevention, they also pose significant threats to civil liberties. Imagine walking down a street where every move is recorded, analyzed, and stored. Although such measures may intend to increase safety, they can easily overstep personal boundaries, leading to situations where individuals feel constantly watched or monitored. This can fundamentally change how people behave in public spaces, potentially stifling freedom of expression and assembly, essential elements of a democratic society.

A related issue is the concept of the "Right to Forget," which advocates for an individual's ability to erase personal data from databases upon request. However, implementing this idea in the realm of AI isn't straightforward. AI systems often rely on interconnected datasets spread across various platforms and networks. Removing all traces of one's personal information is almost like trying to gather scattered feathers in the wind. Even if a company complies with a deletion request, backups and third-party entities possessing the same data can complicate the process. This creates a scenario where personal information continues to linger, accessible to unauthorized parties and used without explicit consent.

Transparency emerges as a critical component to address these challenges. Users need to know what data is being collected, how it's being used, and by whom. For instance, AI algorithms in social media platforms often collect user activity to tailor content feeds. But how many users genuinely understand this process? Making AI systems transparent involves presenting data collection policies in clear language, not buried within pages of legal jargon. It's about shifting power back to the user, ensuring that they are informed participants rather than passive subjects in data collection schemes.

Beyond transparency, informed consent stands as another pillar of ethical data usage. People should have the autonomy to decide whether they agree with the terms of data handling. This means offering clear choices before data is collected, allowing individuals to opt-in knowingly. Consider an app requesting location access—what if users could specify that the app only tracks them during work hours or weekends? Providing these options educates individuals on data usage and empowers them to manage their own privacy actively.

Furthermore, the risks of data breaches and unauthorized usage cannot be overlooked. In an era where cyber-attacks are increasingly common, AI systems must prioritize secure data storage and robust protection measures. The fallout of a breach can be devastating, leading to identity theft, financial loss, and erosion of trust in technological systems. Addressing these vulnerabilities requires continuous updates to security protocols, investment in cybersecurity technologies, and most importantly, accountability from organizations handling data.

Bias and Discrimination in AI Algorithms

Bias in AI systems has emerged as a pressing concern due to its wide-reaching societal implications. These biases often originate from the datasets used to train AI models. When we input data that reflects societal prejudices or historical injustices, AI systems can inadvertently learn and replicate these biases. For example, if a dataset primarily comprises information from a particular demographic group while neglecting others, the AI might develop an inherent bias against underrepresented groups. This can lead to discriminatory outcomes in crucial areas such as hiring, law enforcement, and lending.

The perpetuation of stereotypes by algorithms is another troubling aspect. Algorithms, designed to recognize patterns quickly, can reinforce existing inequalities by continuously associating specific characteristics with certain demographics. For instance, suppose a hiring algorithm frequently selects applicants based on past successful candidates who belong predominantly to one gender or race. In that case, it may overlook equally qualified individuals from different backgrounds. This cycle perpetuates entrenched social disparities, making it challenging for progress towards equality.

To counteract these biases, several strategies are essential. One approach is regular auditing of AI systems. By conducting thorough examinations, developers and stakeholders can identify points where biases may creep in and implement corrective measures. Diverse team involvement is another crucial step. Bringing together individuals from varied backgrounds ensures that multiple perspectives are considered during the development phase. This diversity reduces the risk of blind spots that could lead to unintentional biases, fostering a more inclusive AI landscape.

Moreover, ethical implications and accountability must be at the forefront of AI development. Developers have a responsibility not only to acknowledge the potential biases in their systems but also to proactively address them. This involves being transparent about the sources of data, the decision-making processes within the algorithms, and the testing methods employed to detect biases. It also requires establishing clear accountability structures, ensuring that there are consequences when biases result in harm or discrimination. This level of transparency builds trust between AI developers and the communities they serve.

In addition to technical solutions, societal awareness and education play vital roles in combating bias in AI. By increasing public understanding of how AI systems work and how biases can arise, we empower individuals to advocate for fairer, more equitable AI applications. Educational initiatives can demystify AI, making it accessible and relatable, thus encouraging broader participation in discussions about its ethical use.

Job Displacement Fears Due to AI

In today's rapidly changing technological landscape, one of the most pressing concerns is the potential for AI to displace jobs. This fear is not new; humanity has faced similar anxieties during previous technological revolutions. For instance, in the 19th century, the Industrial Revolution introduced machines that replaced many manual tasks. Despite initial job losses, new industries and opportunities emerged over time, reshaping the workforce and creating roles that were previously unimaginable. Understanding this historical context can provide valuable insights into how today's job market might transform in response to AI advancements.

Currently, there are several industries where AI-driven automation is already making a significant impact. Manufacturing is perhaps the most visibly affected sector, with robots and automated systems taking over assembly line tasks that once required human hands. The rise of AI in logistics and transportation is another example, where companies explore autonomous vehicles and drones to streamline delivery processes. Moreover, the finance industry increasingly utilizes AI algorithms to perform tasks like fraud detection and risk assessment, which were traditionally handled by teams of analysts. As these technologies continue to evolve, it's not just blue-collar jobs that are at risk; white-collar positions too might see changes as AI takes on more complex decision-making roles.

Looking to the future, we must consider the broader implications of AI on the workforce. While certain jobs may become obsolete, others will emerge that require different skills and expertise. This shift underscores the necessity for reskilling and adaptation among the current workforce. Educational institutions and employers alike have a role to play in this transition. By providing training opportunities and fostering a culture of lifelong learning, we can help individuals adjust to the evolving demands of the job market. For example, programs focusing on digital literacy, data analysis, and AI management could empower workers to thrive in an AI-integrated economy.

Another aspect to consider is the importance of policy changes and discussions regarding future work dynamics. Policymakers need to address the challenges posed by AI-induced job displacement with comprehensive strategies that promote economic stability and social welfare. One approach could involve implementing safety nets such as universal basic income or job transition funds to support those affected by automation. Additionally, encouraging public-private partnerships can facilitate the development of new industries and create job opportunities in emerging sectors. Such collaborative efforts will be essential for ensuring that the benefits of AI progress are broadly shared across society.

Moreover, conversations about the future of work should actively involve diverse stakeholders, including employees, employers, educators, and policymakers. These dialogues can explore various scenarios and devise plans to mitigate potential downsides. It's also crucial to cultivate an open mindset toward AI, recognizing it not as a threat but as a tool that can enhance productivity and innovation if harnessed responsibly.

AI and Accountability: Who is Responsible?

Accountability in AI development and deployment is a complex issue that touches on various ethical, legal, and practical dimensions. As AI systems become more integrated into our daily lives, the question of who is responsible when things go wrong becomes increasingly pressing. When an AI system causes harm, either through error or malicious use, pinpointing responsibility isn't straightforward. Is it the developer who wrote the code, the company that provided the data, or perhaps the user who deployed the system? Moreover, AI systems are often designed to learn and adapt beyond the initial programming, adding another layer of complexity to attribution.

This uncertainty can create legal and moral ambiguities. Current legal frameworks, largely built for traditional human-led activities, struggle to accommodate the nuances of AI technologies. Many laws were not crafted with autonomous decision-making agents in mind, leaving gaps in accountability. For instance, if an AI-guided car makes an erroneous decision leading to an accident, traditional liability laws might not adequately address this scenario. Reforming these frameworks to cater specifically to AI is essential. Legal experts suggest developing new statutes or modifying existing ones to consider the unique characteristics of AI systems. For example, introducing regulations that require a clear chain of responsibility from developers to users could be one way forward.

In parallel, explainable AI offers a pathway to enhance transparency and understanding. Explainable AI refers to systems that provide clear, human-readable explanations for their decisions and actions. This is crucial because, without such clarity, it's difficult to determine what went wrong when an AI makes an unexpected choice. Transparency can also help demystify AI processes, making them more understandable and acceptable to the general public. Users are more likely to trust a system they understand. Guidelines for implementing transparency include documenting algorithms' decision paths and ensuring they are accessible for audits.

Moreover, fostering public engagement in AI developments is vital for building trust and ensuring ethical practices. Public involvement does not necessarily mean developing technical expertise but rather providing feedback and participating in discussions about how AI should be used and governed. In recent years, initiatives that involve stakeholders, including consumers, in AI ethics discussions have gained prominence. These initiatives may take the form of public forums, consultations, and collaborative projects between AI developers and communities.

By engaging with the public, developers can align their projects with societal values and expectations, which is critical for ensuring technologies benefit everyone. It also means developers and policymakers need to listen actively to concerns raised by non-specialists since they bring fresh perspectives that might not be apparent within tech circles.

It's important to recognize that achieving accountability in AI is not a task for one entity alone. It requires a collective effort involving governments, industries, academia, and civil society. Governments can set the tone by creating regulatory environments that encourage responsible AI innovation while protecting consumers and citizens from potential harms. Companies can prioritize ethical considerations in their business models and product designs, setting standards for others to follow.

Regulation Frameworks for Ethical AI Use

Navigating the landscape of AI regulation is like trying to hit a moving target—new technologies emerge rapidly, outpacing existing regulatory frameworks. First on our journey is a review of the primary regulations that currently govern AI use. Many countries have taken steps to establish legal guidelines. However, these are often piecemeal efforts that may not offer comprehensive coverage. In some cases, laws were enacted before AI's rise and do not address specific issues like decision-making transparency or accountability when AI systems fail. For example, the EU's General Data Protection Regulation (GDPR) touches upon automated decision-making but leaves many questions unanswered about AI's expanding role.

The complexity grows as we compare how different regions approach AI regulation. The European Union, China, and the United States each present unique strategies, reflecting distinct cultural and political philosophies. The EU takes a proactive stance with proposals like the AI Act, aiming for robust human oversight. Conversely, the US prefers industry self-regulation, focusing on innovation rather than restriction. Meanwhile, China adopts a heavy-handed approach that aligns with its more centralized governance model. Looking at successful case studies, we find Singapore's balanced framework noteworthy. It combines clear guidelines with incentives for responsible AI use, setting an example worth emulating.

Proposing a comprehensive ethical framework involves engaging diverse stakeholders, including government bodies, tech companies, academics, and civil society groups. Each brings vital insights and priorities to the table. Governments can legislate, but without industry support and adherence, policy changes are ineffective. Similarly, academic researchers provide essential evidence-based recommendations, while civil society organizations highlight public concerns and potential rights infringements. A collaborative framework ensures that all voices are heard and integrated into the AI ethics dialogue. This cooperation is crucial in developing guidelines that are both practical and enforceable.

As AI technology evolves, so too do the challenges it presents. Anticipating these emerging challenges means staying alert to new developments that could bypass current regulations. Consider the growth of AI in fields like healthcare or autonomous vehicles, which introduce unprecedented risks and benefits. These advancements call for adaptive regulations capable of evolving alongside technological progress. One key area is data privacy, where dynamic regulatory models might be required to address the sophisticated ways personal data gets used and shared by AI systems.

To build resilience against unforeseen risks, a flexible regulatory approach is necessary. Traditional rule-making methods—often slow and cumbersome—might not suffice in dealing with AI's pace. Instead, policymakers should adopt iterative processes that allow continuous updates. Regulatory sandboxes, for example, offer controlled environments where new AI technologies can be tested under real-world conditions without permanent exposure to existing rigid regulations. This adaptability helps identify potential issues early, providing room for swift corrective measures and minimizing negative impacts on society.

Moreover, crafting a global consensus on AI ethics is a formidable task but imperative. While regional differences exist, there is a universal agreement on key principles: AI systems should respect human rights, promote fairness, and maintain transparency. International forums and collaborations, such as the OECD's AI Principles, are instrumental in harmonizing standards across borders. They provide a platform for sharing best practices and aligning on core values, ensuring AI development does not compromise human dignity or autonomy.

At the heart of effective AI regulation is the need for education and awareness. Policymakers, developers, and users alike must understand the ethical considerations involved. Training programs and public awareness campaigns can empower all parties to engage meaningfully in discussions about AI's future. This informed dialogue is essential for fostering trust in AI systems and mitigating fears associated with their deployment. After all, regulation is not solely about restriction; it's about enabling safe, innovative, and socially beneficial AI applications.

Insights and Implications

We've explored some big themes in this chapter, like privacy concerns and the tricky ethics of AI. From data collection to surveillance systems, it's clear that as AI becomes a bigger part of our lives, we need to think carefully about who has access to our information and how they use it. It's not just about understanding what's happening with our data but also about making sure we're okay with it. That's where transparency and informed consent come in. If people know what data is being collected and have control over its use, it empowers them to protect their privacy better.

On top of privacy, we've dived into how bias in AI can lead to discrimination. When AI systems learn from flawed data, they can end up reinforcing stereotypes or making unfair decisions. Tackling these biases requires effort—from auditing systems to involving diverse voices in AI development. The responsibility doesn't just fall on developers; it's a whole community effort involving policymakers, educators, and everyday users. By staying informed and engaged, we can work toward an ethical framework for AI that considers everyone's rights and opportunities. It's crucial that we keep these conversations going to ensure AI benefits are shared widely and responsibly.

Chapter 8

AI as a Tool for Creativity

U sing AI as a tool for creativity is reshaping how we think about art and innovation. Gone are the days when only those with formal training could create compelling artworks or compose intricate music. Nowadays, AI platforms like DALL-E and AIVA are revolutionizing creativity by making it more accessible to everyone. These tools allow people to explore new creative territories without needing traditional skills. Imagine typing a description of an image you want to bring to life, and voila! An AI program turns your words into a stunning piece of digital art. This isn't just about producing art; it's about expanding what we think is possible in artistic creation. With AI, anyone can be an artist or composer, offering fresh perspectives that challenge our notions of originality and authorship.

In this chapter, we're diving into some exciting ways AI is transforming creative fields. We'll explore how AI-generated art and music are pushing boundaries, turning novice creators into artists and musicians. You'll see how these tools are sparking debates about what creativity truly means and how they're redefining our understanding of art and music. We'll delve into how AI is not just a tool but also a collaborator, assisting artists and musicians in broadening their horizons while saving time. From there, we'll touch on AI's role in curating and enhancing user engagement, converting passive viewers into active participants in the storytelling process. Lastly, we'll discuss how these advancements pave the way for collaborations that transcend geographical and skill-related barriers, inviting new conversations about inspiration and authenticity. By the end, you'll gain a glimpse into a world where technology and creativity meet, creating opportunities for even more innovative expressions.

AI-generated Art and Music

In today's rapidly evolving technological landscape, artificial intelligence is increasingly being recognized as a potent tool for creativity. Traditionally, art and music have been domains where human creativity thrived, driven by emotion, culture, and personal expression. However, with the advent of innovative AI tools like DALL-E and MidJourney, the barrier to entry for creating unique visual artworks has significantly lowered. These platforms allow individuals who may not possess formal artistic training to explore their creative potential by generating personalized images from text prompts. This democratization of art creation is revolutionizing the way we perceive authorship and originality in the digital era.

Imagine sitting at your computer, typing a description of an image you envision—a serene sunset with vibrant hues of orange and pink mingling with towering purple clouds. With tools like DALL-E, this description transforms into a digital artwork, capturing nuances that might be challenging even for seasoned artists. Such technology empowers users, giving them a canvas to manifest their imaginations without requiring technical expertise in traditional art forms. This phenomenon sparks conversations about how AI blurs the lines between artist and tool, prompting debates on the true essence of creativity.

Similarly, in the realm of music, AI platforms are pushing the boundaries of composition. Software like AIVA, which stands for Artificial Intelligence Virtual Artist, plays a pivotal role in assisting musicians. By leveraging vast libraries of musical influences, AIVA generates diverse compositions that musicians can refine and adapt to their unique styles. Consider an aspiring composer overwhelmed by the prospect of arranging a symphony; with AIVA's assistance, they can explore unconventional harmonies and rhythms, broadening their creative horizons. This software not only saves time but also encourages experimentation, inviting creators to venture outside their comfort zones and explore uncharted musical territories.

Additionally, AI systems equipped with sophisticated algorithms are redefining how we experience art curation. These algorithms analyze existing works of art, assessing patterns, styles, and trends. By doing so, they suggest novel approaches to art, helping curators develop exhibitions that resonate more deeply with audiences. The dynamic interactions facilitated by such algorithms enhance user engagement, turning passive viewers into active participants in the storytelling process. Art is no longer confined to static displays; it becomes an evolving dialogue where AI introduces fresh perspectives and challenges traditional norms.

A striking example of AI's transformative power in art lies in projects like Google's DeepDream. This initiative uses deep neural networks to create images that are often surreal and dream-like, distorting familiar objects in ways that challenge our perception of reality. The results are visually stunning yet provoke thought about what defines art. By creating neural network distortions, DeepDream promotes discussions regarding aesthetic standards and forces us to reevaluate our understanding of beauty. These tech-induced dialogues open new pathways for artists and art lovers to engage with creativity, fostering a deeper appreciation for the marriage between technology and art.

While AI's potential to augment creativity is immense, it's essential to approach its integration thoughtfully. For many, the blending of human intuition with machine efficiency represents a compelling partnership. Humans contribute emotional depth, context, and cultural insights that machines lack, whereas AI provides swift data processing and pattern recognition capabilities. Together, they form a synergy that enhances both the artistic process and the final product.

AI's role in transforming creative sectors extends beyond merely offering tools and suggestions. It invites a paradigm shift in how we conceive creativity itself. One intriguing aspect is how these technologies stimulate debates around ownership, inspiration, and authenticity. When an AI-generated piece wins an art competition or charts as a musical hit, questions arise: Who truly deserves credit? Is it the algorithm's developers or the individuals who inputted the creative commands?

Furthermore, AI's impact on creativity is evident in its ability to inspire collaboration. Projects that once seemed impossible due to geographical, temporal, or skill-related constraints are now feasible. Musicians across continents can collaborate in real-time, artists can build on each other's work seamlessly, and ideas multiply through shared digital canvases. Technology acts as a bridge, connecting diverse creative minds and facilitating a richer exchange of ideas and cultures.

Despite skepticism, AI's capacity to innovate within artistic realms is undeniable. As we navigate this complex interplay between technology and human creativity, embracing AI as a collaborator rather than a competitor offers exciting possibilities. Lessons learned from AI-assisted creations highlight that innovation thrives when diverse talents converge—human and artificial alike—pushing the boundaries of what's conceivable.

Enhancement of Creative Writing with AI

In the world of writing, AI has become a powerful ally. From aspiring writers to seasoned authors, the tools provided by artificial intelligence can significantly enhance the creative process. Let's delve into how AI assists writers from the initial stages of brainstorming to the final edits.

Starting with one of the most prevalent AI applications, writing assistants like Grammarly have revolutionized how we approach grammar and style. These tools offer more than just spelling corrections; they provide comprehensive suggestions for improving sentence structure, word choice, and overall tone. For non-writers or those who may lack confidence in their grammatical skills, this means that polished work is now within reach without extensive training. By analyzing vast databases of language usage, these assistants can suggest alterations that make text clearer and more engaging, democratizing the editing process and enabling anyone to produce content that feels professional.

But AI doesn't stop at correcting what you've already written. It also plays a crucial role in overcoming writer's block, a common hurdle for many. Generative AI tools offer endless prompts and outlines tailored to various genres and themes. Imagine staring at a blank page, unsure where to begin, and then accessing an AI tool that provides the inspiration needed to start writing. Whether it's a first sentence, a plot twist, or a new character idea, these tools help spark creativity, encouraging writers to explore diverse thematic explorations they might not have considered otherwise. They offer the freedom to experiment and take risks, knowing there's a supportive tool ready to guide them back on track if needed.

Moreover, there's the growing trend of using AI for automated content creation. Businesses, particularly in the digital realm, require a constant stream of content to engage audiences and maintain visibility. AI-powered platforms can generate articles, reports, and other types of business content quickly and efficiently. This capability raises questions about the future role of professional writers. While AI can handle repetitive tasks and data-driven content production, it challenges us to consider the authentic human touch in storytelling and nuanced communication. The efficiency AI brings in producing bulk content is undeniable, but it also invites us to question what aspects of writing are inherently human and irreplaceable.

The journey doesn't end there. AI facilitates collaborative storytelling through co-writing tools, allowing writers to explore narrative elements more deeply. These tools can suggest plot developments, dialogue options, or even entire chapters based on existing material. By interacting with AI in this way, writers can engage in a dynamic exchange of ideas, testing different narrative paths and outcomes. This collaboration enriches the storytelling experience, not only for the creators but for the audience as well. Users become part of the story, influencing its progression, which enhances engagement and makes the narrative feel more alive and interactive.

AI in Film-making and Special Effects

In the world of filmmaking, AI has emerged as a revolutionary tool that is reshaping how stories are told on the big screen. Traditionally, crafting a successful script involved a combination of creativity and intuition, often aiming to tap into audience desires with limited data for guidance. However, today, advancements in AI are changing this dynamic. By analyzing thousands of successful scripts, AI systems can identify trends and patterns, offering invaluable insights into market demands and audience preferences. This means writers can develop scripts with a more informed approach, tailoring their storytelling to maximize impact and appeal.

Moreover, AI's transformative influence extends beyond just scriptwriting. In the realm of visual effects, AI technologies have brought about a significant change in creating realistic computer-generated imagery (CGI). Previously, creating lifelike CGI was an arduous task requiring immense time and resources. Now, AI can reduce production times significantly while enhancing quality. For instance, techniques such as digitally de-aging actors have become more streamlined with AI, enabling filmmakers to explore new storytelling avenues and revive characters from different eras seamlessly within the narrative.

Editing, another crucial component of filmmaking, has also seen a paradigm shift due to AI integration. Editing tasks that were once labor-intensive and consumed countless hours are now automated through AI tools. By handling these repetitive tasks, AI allows filmmakers to focus on their broader vision and creative expression. This newfound freedom encourages directors and editors to experiment with innovative styles and sequences, pushing the boundaries of conventional filmmaking without being bogged down by technical constraints.

Furthermore, in the ever-evolving landscape of media consumption, reaching the right audience effectively is crucial. AI optimizes audience reach and marketing strategies through sophisticated data analysis. It evaluates trends across diverse demographics, guiding filmmakers and marketers in crafting targeted campaigns. This not only enhances engagement but also aids in planning distribution strategies that ensure content reaches audiences who will appreciate it the most. With

AI's assistance, decisions regarding release formats, promotional tactics, and content placements become more data-driven and precise.

AI's role in transforming filmmaking isn't solely about technical enhancements—it's about enriching the entire creative process. By bridging the gap between human creativity and machine efficiency, AI serves as both enhancer and collaborator. Filmmakers can harness its capabilities to translate their visions into reality more vividly and compellingly than ever before. Through AI, filmmakers are empowered to craft narratives that resonate deeply with audiences worldwide, intertwining technology and artistry in profound ways.

Supporting Design and Architecture through AI

AI has become a revolutionary force in design and architecture, offering new ways to unlock creativity and innovation. Let's explore how AI is reshaping these fields, starting with the use of generative design algorithms. These algorithms are like digital brainstorming partners that suggest numerous design options based on specified parameters. They go beyond traditional methods by considering both functionality and aesthetics. For instance, architects can input requirements for a building, such as dimensions, materials, and environmental conditions, and the AI will generate a variety of designs to choose from. This method opens up possibilities that might have been overlooked otherwise and encourages designers to think outside the box.

Moving forward, AI software significantly enhances 3D modeling and simulation in architectural projects. By providing real-time renderings, architects can visualize changes instantly, which speeds up the decision-making process. Additionally, AI contributes to improving energy efficiency and spatial planning. It can simulate how different design elements, like windows or walls, affect energy consumption, allowing for more sustainable buildings. An example of this is using AI to analyze sunlight patterns throughout the year, informing decisions about window placement to maximize natural lighting and reduce electricity use. These advancements make the design process not only faster but also smarter, focusing on long-term sustainability.

In urban planning, AI plays a crucial role in optimizing development and resource allocation. By analyzing data on population growth, traffic patterns, and resource availability, AI models help city officials plan for future needs. This analytical power supports the creation of sustainable communities, where infrastructure grows in harmony with its residents' demands. Cities like Singapore and Barcelona have already implemented AI-driven smart systems for traffic management and water distribution, showcasing practical, positive impacts. Such technology enables planners to foresee potential challenges and address them proactively, ensuring cities remain livable and efficient in the face of change.

Moreover, AI facilitates data-driven design feedback, bridging gaps between client visions and functional outcomes. Traditionally, there might be a disconnect between what clients envision and what is practically feasible. However, with AI, designers receive continuous feedback based on real-world usage data. This ongoing loop allows adjustments to be made even after the design is implemented, ensuring it meets users' needs efficiently. For example, in office spaces, sensors could collect data on areas frequently used versus those that aren't, suggesting alterations to improve functionality or comfort. This adaptability helps maintain relevance in designs, fostering satisfaction among end-users.

As we see, AI infuses creativity into design and architecture by taking on repetitive tasks and offering new insights. It's not about replacing human creativity but enhancing it, enabling professionals to push boundaries further than ever before. While some may worry about AI taking jobs, it's important to recognize how it actually complements human skills, allowing designers and architects to focus on more innovative aspects of their work.

Collaborative Creativity between Humans and AI

In the ever-evolving landscape of creativity, one fascinating synergy has emerged between human creators and artificial intelligence (AI). This collaboration isn't about AI replacing human ingenuity; rather, it's about enhancing and expanding the creative process through diverse approaches. Imagine this: individuals across various creative fields are utilizing AI tools as partners in their artistic endeavors. From visual arts to music composition, these tools act as innovative collaborators, opening doors to new possibilities that might not be accessible otherwise.

For instance, artists can employ AI to generate unique design elements or suggest unconventional color palettes, allowing them to push the boundaries of traditional techniques. Musicians might use AI to compose intricate soundscapes or explore genres they haven't tackled before, enriching their work with layers of complexity previously unimaginable. By incorporating AI into their work, creators are not only broadening their own perspectives but also reaching a wider audience who appreciates these novel artistic expressions.

Beyond individual use, AI-powered workshops are transforming communities by fostering engagement and inclusivity in artistic expression. These workshops create spaces where people from different backgrounds can come together, learn, and experiment. Through hands-on sessions, participants gain practical experience in using AI creatively, whether it's generating art with algorithms or experimenting with machine learning models for music production. This communal approach cultivates a sense of belonging, where everyone feels empowered to contribute their unique voice to the creative tapestry. Moreover, these workshops have been instrumental in breaking down barriers, making technology more approachable for those who might initially be hesitant about its implications.

Importantly, AI systems themselves continue to evolve through feedback loops established by user interactions. Every interaction provides valuable data that AI learns and adapts from, resulting in more enriched and relevant creative content. Consider an AI tool used by writers to develop plot ideas—over time, as it analyzes user preferences and suggestions, it becomes adept at offering more personalized and compelling storylines. This continuous learning process reinforces the notion that AI isn't just passively supporting creativity but actively shaping the way it unfolds.

Historical case studies offer concrete examples of successful human-AI collaborations, illustrating AI's potential as a partner in innovation. Take, for example, the partnership between filmmakers and AI in developing cutting-edge visual effects for movies. AI-assisted tools have revolutionized how scenes are crafted, enabling filmmakers to realize their visions with greater precision and efficiency. Similarly, AI's role in fashion design has led to groundbreaking trends, where designers leverage algorithms to predict future styles and fabrics that resonate with consumers globally.

Such projects highlight the harmonious blend of human intuition and AI's computational prowess, showcasing a future where both can coexist productively. We've already seen instances where AI-generated art has garnered attention in prestigious galleries, prompting discussions about originality and authorship. Far from being a replacement, AI serves as a medium through which human creativity can be expressed in ways that may not have been possible before.

While some may remain skeptical about integrating AI into creative processes, the benefits of this collaboration are hard to overlook. It's important to remember that AI, when used thoughtfully, is a tool—a bridge connecting human potential with technological advancement. By embracing this partnership, we're not only preserving our creative heritage but also paving the way for future innovations that honor tradition while exploring uncharted territories.

Concluding Thoughts

Throughout the chapter, we've journeyed through the fascinating ways AI is reshaping the landscape of creativity. From revolutionizing art and music to enhancing writing and filmmaking, AI stands as a potent collaborator, opening up creative realms once considered exclusive to human touch. For those dabbling in art, AI tools like DALL-E are not just lowering barriers; they're inviting everyone to engage with artistic expression and redefine what makes something original. Meanwhile, in music, AI's presence encourages musicians to explore new genres with ease, allowing them to break free from traditional constraints and dive into unfamiliar waters. This chapter showcases AI's ability to democratize creativity, making it accessible and inclusive for anyone willing to explore its potential.

AI doesn't just stop at assisting individuals; it thrives on collaboration, bringing people together who might never have met otherwise. Whether it's writers overcoming blocks or filmmakers crafting vivid scenes, AI has become an integral part of modern storytelling and design. It's about blending human intuition with machine precision, creating synergies that push the boundaries of what's possible. As you ponder the tech-driven artscapes discussed here, consider the broader implications for your own field or interests. The take-home message? Embracing AI doesn't mean losing our spark of creativity—quite the opposite. It means expanding our horizons and exploring the richer tapestries of what we can achieve together.

Chapter 9

AI Myths Debunked

U nraveling AI myths involves diving into a world full of misconceptions and exaggerated claims about what artificial intelligence can actually do. It's easy to get swept away with ideas of futuristic robots or machines that think and feel just like humans. Yet, the truth about AI is much more grounded and practical than science fiction would have us believe. Machines aren't ready to take over the world or replace all human jobs overnight. Instead, they're tools created to enhance our daily lives, handle specific tasks, and help solve problems more efficiently without ever truly understanding emotion or intent. The allure of AI lies in its ability to perform complex computations and analyze vast datasets with speed, but this doesn't equate to them having minds or feelings of their own.

This chapter will shed light on some common misunderstandings surrounding AI, such as the belief that AI is synonymous with those humanoid robots we often see in movies. It dives into how AI, instead of acting as independent entities, operates under human oversight and the parameters defined by programmers. We'll explore distinctions between narrow AI and the elusive concept of general intelligence, emphasizing that what we really interact with today are systems designed for specific tasks. You'll gain insight into how AI's influence extends quietly throughout our software-driven world—not through dramatic robotic figures but via algorithms behind email filters, recommendation systems, and even virtual assistants. Furthermore, the discussion addresses employment fears, clarifying that while AI might transform certain roles, it also opens doors to new opportunities. By demystifying these concepts, the chapter aims to provide a more balanced view of AI's potential, challenges, and how it fits into everyday life in a way that's far less intimidating and much more exciting than one might initially imagine.

AI is not synonymous with human-like robots

When most people think of artificial intelligence, their minds often drift toward images of humanoid robots resembling those from science fiction movies. However, the reality is far more nuanced and ubiquitous. AI's influence extends beyond these cinematic representations into a multitude of non-robotic applications that shape our daily experiences. One significant area where AI manifests itself extensively is within software applications. These are tools we use every day, perhaps without even realizing the role AI plays behind the scenes.

For instance, chatbots have emerged as a quintessential example of AI in action. They assist with customer service, answer queries, and provide information tailored to user needs. While engaging with them may feel like chatting with a helpful assistant, the underlying technology is a sophisticated form of AI that learns from interactions to improve over time. Similarly, recommendation systems are pervasive in online spaces, like the suggestions you see on streaming services or shopping platforms. Whether it's recommending the next movie to watch based on your viewing history or suggesting products related to previous purchases, AI algorithms analyze vast amounts of data to predict what might interest you most.

These software-driven applications demonstrate how AI simplifies and enhances our digital experiences. Yet many of us use these tools daily without recognizing the AI engine powering them. This underscores a vital point: AI doesn't always wear a face or come with a robot body. It thrives quietly but impactfully within the software realm, transforming how industries operate and interact with customers.

Beyond specific tools like chatbots and recommendation systems, AI seamlessly integrates into everyday software that many individuals rely on, whether for personal or professional tasks. Consider email filtering systems that weed out spam or prioritize important messages. These systems employ AI to learn user preferences and adapt their sorting mechanisms accordingly to maintain an efficient inbox experience.

Further emphasizing AI's invisibility in everyday life is its presence in navigation apps, which optimize routes based on traffic conditions by learning from patterns and real-time data. Fitness applications use AI to track activities and offer personalized workout recommendations, while virtual voice assistants like Siri or Alexa streamline tasks through natural language processing, interpreting spoken commands to set reminders, control smart devices, or play music.

Such examples illustrate how people encounter AI almost unconsciously in their daily routines. The beauty lies in how unobtrusively AI integrates into our environments, quietly improving efficiency and personalized user experiences. Despite lacking physical form, these interactions highlight how deeply embedded AI has become in everyday technology.

Focusing on the technological foundation of AI further clarifies its diverse nature beyond robotics. Much of AI's prowess resides in algorithms and data analysis—areas often overshadowed by more tangible manifestations. Algorithms act as the brains behind AI, processing information, identifying patterns, and making decisions based on data input. They are crafted meticulously to manage specific tasks, iterating on accumulated insights to enhance performance continuously.

Data analysis, another cornerstone of AI, involves sifting through massive datasets to provide meaningful interpretations crucial for informed decision-making. For companies, this means leveraging AI to detect consumer behavior trends, forecast market demands, or optimize operational efficiencies. For scientists and researchers, it opens avenues for breakthroughs by analyzing complex datasets efficiently—be it understanding climate patterns or advancing medical research.

By concentrating on these foundational aspects, one appreciates AI's extensive reach beyond physical embodiments. The powerful combination of sophisticated algorithms and comprehensive data analyses propels advancements across sectors, underscoring the versatile applicability of AI. As industries continue to evolve, embracing these capabilities can foster innovation and create opportunities previously unimaginable.

Understanding AI's multifaceted existence allows us to move away from limiting perceptions tied solely to humanoid robots. Recognizing its widespread adoption in software applications, daily encounters, and algorithmic processes opens avenues for appreciating AI's true potential. Encouragingly, this perspective invites everyone—from the curious bystander to the skeptical observer—to engage with AI discussions more openly, fostering a balanced appreciation of technology's role in shaping modern living.

Understanding AI vs. General Intelligence

Artificial Intelligence, often conjured in popular imagination as futuristic machines with human-like abilities, is actually a broad field with distinct levels of development. To truly understand AI, it's crucial to distinguish between narrow AI and the elusive concept of general intelligence—two realms that are entirely different in their current states and capabilities.

Narrow AI, which is what we predominantly encounter today, refers to systems designed to carry out specific tasks. These include language processing, like the chatbots you might interact with online, or recommendation algorithms suggesting what movie to watch next on your favorite streaming platform. Narrow AI excels at these tasks because it's built with highly specialized rules and data sets that allow it to perform within set boundaries efficiently. However, this type of AI lacks the ability to apply its knowledge outside its predefined area of expertise. For instance, an algorithm managing stock trading can't switch roles and suddenly become adept at medical diagnostics. This lack of versatile adaptability is one of the fundamental limitations of narrow AI. Although extremely proficient within its scope, it doesn't possess comprehensive understanding or reasoning beyond its programmed domain.

In contrast, when we talk about general intelligence, we're referring to a form of AI that would exhibit human-like reasoning, learning, and problem-solving across various contexts without needing task-specific programming. Such an AI could conceivably understand a joke, solve a complex scientific query, and then assist in designing user-friendly software—all without distinct directives for each activity. It's a level of cognitive flexibility found in humans, who naturally adapt knowledge and experience to new situations. As of now, general intelligence remains an unachieved frontier in AI research. Despite the advances in machine learning and neural networks, no existing AI can genuinely replicate the expansive and dynamic thought processes inherent to human beings.

Historically, we've seen vast differences between human intellect and the state of artificial intelligence. Human brains have evolved over millions of years, equipped not only with cognitive abilities but also with emotional depth, intuition, and social understanding. This complexity has not been mirrored in machines, which operate from logical frameworks and datasets rather than introspective consciousness or emotional comprehension. The gap between human and machine intellect underscores the limitations of AI today. Our technology might be able to beat the world's best chess players, yet it struggles with open-ended challenges that demand genuine creativity, empathy, or moral judgment—areas where humans continue to excel.

Looking into the future, it's easy to get caught up in dramatic predictions about AI surpassing human intellect or taking over our daily lives. However, while some advancements suggest exciting possibilities, they also present risks that are sometimes exaggerated in public discourse. It's critical to maintain a balanced perspective. The fear of an impending AI-dominated dystopia often overshadows the practical benefits AI can bring when appropriately harnessed. Researchers continue to push the envelope, exploring how AI might learn with greater independence or engage more naturally in conversational contexts. Nevertheless, the leap from narrow AI to true general intelligence is monumental and unlikely to occur overnight.

The Myth of AI Replacing All Jobs

Artificial intelligence often stirs up concerns about job displacement, leaving many people worried about how AI might impact their careers. However, it's important to understand that while AI does transform jobs by automating certain tasks, it also leads to the creation of new roles and opportunities. Instead of viewing AI as a replacement for human jobs, we should see it as a tool that reshapes the employment landscape.

Job transformation is one of the key aspects of AI's impact on employment. With advancements in technology, some repetitive tasks are now handled by AI, allowing employees to focus on more complex and creative aspects of their work. For instance, customer service bots handle routine inquiries, freeing up time for human agents to tackle more involved customer needs. This shift not only enhances efficiency but also provides workers with opportunities to develop skills in areas that require higher-level thinking and problem-solving.

With these changes come the emergence of completely new roles in industries driven by AI development and implementation. As AI technologies evolve, there is an increasing demand for professionals skilled in data analysis, machine learning, and AI maintenance. These roles are critical for ensuring that AI systems operate smoothly and efficiently. Take, for example, the role of a machine learning engineer, a position that didn't exist a couple of decades ago. Today, such roles are vital for developing algorithms that power AI applications across various sectors.

The historical context provides valuable insights into the current situation. Throughout history, technological advances have consistently altered job landscapes. From the Industrial Revolution to the digital age, each era of innovation has initially sparked fear of job losses, only to demonstrate that technology creates new types of work. When factories first introduced machines, many worried about mass unemployment. Yet, those machines led to increased productivity, economic growth, and ultimately, more jobs in manufacturing and other industries. The parallel with AI is evident; while it may displace certain types of jobs, it also facilitates the creation of new ones.

Moreover, AI can significantly augment productivity. By taking over tedious and time-consuming tasks, AI enables humans to focus on strategic, imaginative, and interpersonal aspects of their work. For example, AI in healthcare can automate administrative duties like scheduling appointments or managing patient records, allowing medical professionals to dedicate more time to patient care and research. This increase in productivity doesn't just benefit individual workers—it can elevate entire organizations' efficiency and output.

A critical element in understanding the impact of AI on jobs is distinguishing between job transformation and job replacement. While automation might eradicate some specific tasks, it doesn't necessarily eliminate entire roles. Instead, AI transforms existing jobs by adjusting the tasks within them. For example, journalists today use AI tools to analyze large datasets quickly, enabling them to uncover stories hidden in the numbers that would be impossible to find manually. Thus, rather than replacing journalists, AI empowers them to do their jobs better and faster.

There's a guideline to keep in mind here: embracing continuous learning and adaptability is crucial for thriving in an AI-enhanced workforce. Workers should be encouraged to acquire new skills and explore interdisciplinary fields where AI plays a role. Engaging in lifelong learning not only helps individuals stay relevant but also ensures they are prepared to fill emerging roles that AI will continue to create. Employers, governments, and educational institutions must support skill development initiatives to facilitate this transition.

The future of work will likely be characterized by collaboration between humans and machines, creating a synergy where AI assists rather than competes against human workers. This collaboration is already visible in many industries. In retail, AI-driven inventory management systems predict restocking needs, helping workers ensure shelves are always stocked with what customers want. This cooperation between AI and human staff improves both service quality and business performance.

To help address concerns around job security, it's essential to foster an open dialogue about AI's impact on employment, involving all stakeholders—employees, employers, policymakers, and technologists. By working together, these groups can guide AI development in ways that are beneficial to the workforce. According to a report from the World Economic Forum, automation is expected to create 133 million new roles globally while displacing 75 million jobs. Such predictions highlight the net positive potential of AI when managed thoughtfully and inclusively.

It's natural for people to be apprehensive about how AI might change their work lives, but there's much to be optimistic about too. As AI continues to integrate into various facets of our professional environments, it brings with it a wealth of new possibilities. By focusing on education, training, and adaptation, society can harness AI's potential to enhance job satisfaction, productivity, and overall economic health.

AI Does Not Operate Independently

Artificial Intelligence (AI) is often imagined as a futuristic entity operating entirely on its own, making decisions with human-like autonomy. However, this view is far from reality. AI systems are not standalone decision-makers; rather, they depend on extensive human oversight to function effectively.

Human oversight is the backbone of AI deployment. It starts with humans curating the data that feeds into these systems. This step is crucial because the quality of input data directly impacts AI performance. If the data is biased or flawed, the AI's outputs will be too. Therefore, humans must meticulously select and interpret data to ensure its relevance and accuracy. Furthermore, human experts frequently review and adjust AI models to refine their accuracy over time, confirming that AI is not left to operate unchecked but is continuously guided by knowledgeable hands.

Next, consider the limitations of AI. Despite impressive advancements in machine learning and artificial intelligence, these systems operate within a framework defined by specific algorithms and parameters set by humans. They lack the ability to independently evolve or change course without explicit programming. This means AI cannot exercise genuine discretion or creativity. For instance, an AI tasked with recognizing images of cats won't suddenly decide to start identifying dogs unless it is reprogrammed to do so. The technical constraints inherent in AI systems highlight the necessity for established guidelines and predetermined paths, ensuring AI remains a tool rather than an autonomous entity.

Another significant aspect is the role of ethical considerations in the realm of AI. Human governance is indispensable in ensuring AI usage aligns with moral values and societal norms. As AI becomes more integrated into various sectors, the potential for misuse or unintended harm grows. Ethical oversight ensures that AI deployments respect privacy rights, avoid discrimination, and contribute positively to society. For example, AI used in hiring processes must be constantly monitored to prevent biases that could lead to unfair treatment of candidates based on race, gender, or other personal attributes. Without rigorous ethical scrutiny, AI systems could inadvertently perpetuate or even exacerbate existing societal inequities.

It's also crucial to emphasize how AI thrives when it works hand-in-hand with human intuition. AI excels at processing massive datasets quickly and spotting patterns that might elude human observation. Yet, when it comes to nuanced decision-making that requires emotional intelligence or creative problem-solving, human input becomes invaluable. Think about how AI aids doctors in diagnosing diseases by quickly analyzing medical data. While AI can point out anomalies more efficiently than a human doctor, it is the doctor's expertise and discernment that ultimately guides the diagnosis and treatment plan. Thus, collaboration between AI and humans leads to outcomes that neither could achieve independently.

The myth of AI's autonomous operation overlooks the vitality of human involvement at every stage—data selection, algorithm design, and continual oversight are all necessary components driven by human expertise. Technical constraints prevent AI from making independent decisions, forcing it to adhere to predefined instructions created by humans. Ethical considerations demand vigilant human governance to ensure AI technologies are deployed responsibly and equitably. And lastly, AI finds its true strength in collaboration with humans, complementing our skills while we supervise its operations.

Why AI Cannot Feel Emotions

In today's world, artificial intelligence (AI) is a hot topic, often portrayed as a technological marvel capable of performing tasks that were once exclusive to humans. However, one common misconception is that AI can comprehend and resonate with human emotions. Let's explore why this belief isn't quite accurate.

Firstly, we need to understand the nature of emotions, which are inherently human. Our feelings are deeply rooted in complex biological processes involving our brain, hormones, and nervous system. They emerge from our personal experiences and interactions with the world around us. Emotions are more than just data; they're imbued with layers of context, history, and consciousness that AI can't replicate. While machines can analyze and process information faster than we ever could, understanding emotions requires a level of depth and subtlety grounded in human biology.

Now, let's talk about how AI operates. Essentially, AI systems are designed to recognize patterns within data through intricate algorithms written by programmers. While AI can mimic certain aspects of emotional expression—such as analyzing facial movements or voice intonations—it only does so based on statistical probabilities rather than genuine understanding. For instance, an AI might be programmed to identify a smile or detect sadness in speech, but it doesn't 'feel' happiness or sorrow itself. These simulations are based on pre-coded responses that lack the essence of true emotional experience.

This distinction between programming and emotion is where things often get confused. People may interact with AI chatbots or virtual assistants that sound empathetic or caring, leading them to believe that these systems possess actual feelings. However, responding empathetically doesn't equate to feeling empathy. It's important to remember that AI merely executes predefined actions or generates responses based on the input it receives. The warmth or concern you perceive is just a facade—a series of calculated outputs determined by algorithms.

The implications of misunderstanding AI's emotional capabilities extend beyond casual interaction. A significant area of concern is its application in emotionally sensitive fields such as therapy or mental health support. Imagine relying on an AI therapist expecting it to provide comfort or understand the nuances of personal struggles. There's potential danger in assigning roles to AI that require authentic emotional exchanges. Recognizing AI's functional limits is crucial in preventing misuse that could lead to adverse outcomes for individuals seeking genuine human connection and understanding.

To navigate these complexities responsibly, it's essential to establish guidelines regarding where and how AI should be deployed in emotional contexts. We must ensure that clearly defined boundaries are in place to differentiate between roles suitable for AI and those that should remain within the human domain. This distinction can prevent scenarios where technology is applied inappropriately, potentially causing harm rather than offering help.

Looking ahead, there are future challenges associated with the misconceptions surrounding AI's emotional understanding. As AI continues to evolve and integrate more into our daily lives, misunderstandings about its capabilities might hinder technological progress or contribute to misuse. If society perceives AI as possessing emotional intelligence akin to humans, we risk blurring the lines between what machines can and cannot do. This confusion might lead to unrealistic expectations and reliance on technology in areas beyond its scope.

Moreover, ethical considerations come into play when determining how we develop and implement AI systems. It is crucial to address potential biases embedded in algorithms, ensuring fairness and accountability. Transparency in how AI decisions are made will foster trust and clarity, helping users better comprehend AI's role and limitations. By educating people on the true nature of AI and its boundaries, we equip them with the knowledge to make informed decisions about its use in various scenarios.

It's important to emphasize that advancing AI shouldn't aim to replace human qualities like empathy or compassion but should focus on complementing human efforts. AI excels in processing vast amounts of information quickly and identifying patterns that might escape a human eye. Utilizing these strengths while respecting the unique attributes of human emotion will allow us to harness AI's potential effectively without overstepping boundaries.

Concluding Thoughts

As we've explored in this chapter, AI isn't just about those sci-fi robots we see in movies. It's much more subtle and integrated into our daily lives. From chatbots helping out with customer service to recommendation systems suggesting your next favorite movie, AI is quietly working behind the scenes. These examples highlight how AI improves efficiency and personalizes experiences without needing to look like a robot. By understanding these everyday applications, it's clear that AI is already an integral part of various industries, enhancing how businesses operate and how we interact with technology.

We've also dived into clarifying the myth that AI will replace all jobs, showing instead how it transforms roles and creates new opportunities. While it automates some tasks, it frees humans to focus on creativity and complex problem-solving, leading to new career paths. Additionally, AI doesn't work independently; it relies on human oversight for data input and ethical guidance. This partnership between humans and machines showcases how they can complement each other's strengths. Understanding AI's true nature allows us to appreciate its impact realistically, paving the way for more informed discussions about how it shapes our future.

Chapter 10

Future Trends in AI Development

A rtificial Intelligence (AI) is set to change our world in incredible ways. It's not just about self-driving cars or smart assistants anymore; AI is making its way into almost every part of our lives, from the way we work and play to how our societies function. As we look to the future, we're beginning to see extraordinary trends in AI development that promise to revolutionize everything around us. Imagine a world where machines can learn and adapt faster than ever before, where they can predict outcomes and offer solutions to problems yet to arise. This chapter explores all these futuristic possibilities, diving into the groundbreaking advancements that AI is heralding in multiple sectors.

In this chapter, we'll take a closer look at the various domains where AI is set to make a huge impact, transforming industries and challenging the way we've done things for decades. We'll delve into the exciting developments in autonomous vehicles, exploring how they're reshaping transportation and urban life. From there, we'll travel beyond our planet, examining AI's role in space exploration and how it helps us gather and analyze vast amounts of data from the universe. Quantum computing is another fascinating area we'll discuss, highlighting the potential breakthroughs it offers when paired with AI. And it's not just technology for tech's sake—AI is stepping up as a critical player in addressing ethical challenges and fighting climate change, ensuring its own evolution aligns with the values and needs of humanity.

Advancements in Autonomous Vehicles

Autonomous vehicles are at the forefront of AI technology's impact on transportation. As AI continues to advance, these vehicles become ever more adept at navigating complex environments, thanks largely to their enhanced perception systems. Imagine a car that can sense its surroundings with pinpoint accuracy, identifying pedestrians, other vehicles, and obstacles in real time. This is made possible by AI algorithms that process data from cameras, radar, and LIDAR sensors. When human error causes over 90% of traffic accidents, the ability of AI-powered vehicles to understand and react instantly can significantly reduce such incidents.

As the technology behind self-driving cars advances, so too must the regulatory frameworks surrounding them. Governments and regulatory bodies worldwide are faced with the critical task of ensuring public safety while fostering innovation. This involves crafting regulations that require thorough testing and validation of autonomous systems before widespread deployment. For example, guidelines might dictate how these vehicles should behave in emergency situations or interact with human-driven cars.

The guidelines for autonomous vehicles also focus on continuous improvement of safety features, which means that vehicles can learn from new data. As these technologies evolve, they are subject to rigorous scrutiny to ensure they meet high safety standards. Establishing legal liability and insurance implications is also part of this evolving landscape. Such frameworks are crucial to building public trust and acceptance, as many people remain wary of relinquishing control to machines.

Beyond just reducing accidents, autonomous vehicles have the potential to transform cityscapes. One of the most exciting prospects is the reduction in the need for parking spaces. In urban areas where space is at a premium, this could lead to significant changes in how land is used. Parking lots might become redundant, making way for green spaces, housing, or commercial developments. The requirement for fewer cars on the road could make cities more pedestrian-friendly and less congested.

Transportation business models could also shift dramatically as these technologies become mainstream. Ride-sharing services are likely to become more prevalent, offering an affordable and convenient alternative to car ownership. Companies might deploy fleets of self-driving taxis, providing transportation-on-demand services without the cost of human drivers. This could disrupt traditional car manufacturers, prompting innovations in how vehicles are produced and marketed to consumers.

In addition to reshaping urban landscapes, AI's role in optimizing traffic management holds promise for environmental sustainability. With smart algorithms directing traffic flow, cities can experience reduced congestion, leading to lower emissions and improved air quality. Intelligent traffic lights, for instance, could adapt in real time to changing conditions, prioritizing routes based on current congestion levels. These improvements contribute directly to pollution reduction initiatives, aligning with global efforts to combat climate change.

By integrating AI into traffic systems, cities can also enhance public transportation networks. Efficient routing and scheduling powered by

AI can make buses and trains more reliable and attractive to commuters, potentially decreasing reliance on personal vehicles. This shift not only supports sustainability goals but also reduces the overall carbon footprint of urban areas.

Furthermore, the environmental benefits of autonomous vehicles extend to energy consumption. With optimized driving patterns and reduced idling, these vehicles can achieve better fuel efficiency compared to conventional cars. As electric vehicles increasingly incorporate self-driving functionalities, there is potential for even greater reductions in greenhouse gas emissions.

While the transformation of transportation through AI brings notable advantages, it also presents challenges that society must address. Issues such as data privacy, cybersecurity, and ethical considerations in decision-making algorithms cannot be ignored. Ensuring that AI systems are transparent and fair will be essential in gaining public confidence and acceptance.

Education and public awareness campaigns play a vital role in demystifying AI and its applications in transportation. By engaging with communities and stakeholders, policymakers can foster open dialogues about the benefits and potential drawbacks of self-driving technology. Sharing success stories and case studies where AI has had a positive impact can help assuage fears and build enthusiasm for its adoption.

Looking ahead, collaboration between government, industry, and academia will be key in shaping the future of AI in transportation. Continuous research and development efforts are necessary to refine technologies and address emerging challenges. By doing so, society can harness the full potential of AI, creating safer, more efficient, and sustainable transportation systems for future generations.

AI in Space Exploration

In the vast expanse of space, artificial intelligence (AI) is beginning to change how we explore and understand the universe. It's no longer just about sending rockets to distant planets; it's also about equipping those missions with intelligent systems that can process massive amounts of data on the fly. These AI systems are essential in today's space expeditions because they can quickly analyze and interpret data while spacecraft are millions of miles away from Earth. This capability not only enhances the efficiency of robotic missions but also allows for real-time decision-making, which is crucial when navigating the unpredictability of space.

Imagine a spacecraft zipping through the void, relaying streams of information back to scientists on Earth. The data collected—ranging from images to temperature readings—can be overwhelming. However, thanks to AI, these spacecraft have onboard systems capable of sifting through this sea of data in seconds. By doing so, they identify key insights and anomalies that might be invisible to the human eye. Such processing power means that missions can adapt and respond to new findings immediately, rather than waiting for instructions from Earth that could take hours or even days to arrive. In essence, AI acts as the brain of these exploratory missions, enabling them to run more smoothly and effectively.

Meanwhile, AI isn't just turning its electronic eyes on our immediate cosmic neighborhood. It's also venturing into the depths of astronomical data, scouring through it to detect patterns and phenomena that might elude traditional methods of analysis. For instance, AI algorithms are making significant strides in recognizing patterns within vast swathes of astronomical data. By doing so, they're able to automatically identify and classify celestial events, such as supernovae or the collision of galaxies. These algorithms work tirelessly, scanning countless images and datasets, highlighting potential objects of interest and freeing up astronomers to focus on interpretation and deeper research.

Moreover, predictive models powered by AI are coming into play by imagining what environments on other worlds are like. These models simulate conditions such as temperature, atmospheric pressure, and surface composition on planets and moons in our solar system and beyond. As a result, these simulations help scientists design better equipment and plan more effective mission strategies. By predicting various environmental scenarios, AI assists researchers in preparing for the unexpected, ensuring that future missions are well-equipped to handle unknowns.

The collaborative nature of AI technologies further amplifies its impact in space exploration. Projects that leverage AI are increasingly becoming a melting pot of ideas and expertise from around the globe. Scientists from different countries and disciplines join forces to push the boundaries of what's possible, sharing knowledge and resources to tackle some of the most pressing challenges in modern space exploration. These collaborations foster international partnerships that pool together a wealth of experience and technology, driving innovation at an unprecedented scale.

For example, satellite missions developed through international cooperation offer intriguing opportunities. Take the partnerships between NASA and the European Space Agency (ESA), where efforts combine to create powerful AI-driven tools and techniques. By aligning goals and methodologies, such partnerships enhance mission outcomes and open new frontiers for discovery. With a shared commitment to exploring beyond our planet, these initiatives harness the full potential of AI, broadening our understanding of the cosmos while strengthening ties between nations.

As AI continues to evolve and embed itself within the intricacies of space exploration, its role is set to grow exponentially. We're only scratching the surface of what's achievable, with many more advancements on the horizon. As these technological innovations unfold, they're likely to redefine our interactions with the universe, offering new ways to discover the unseen and unknown.

What's truly remarkable is the potential for breakthroughs that these AI applications hold. They not only streamline current missions but also pave the way for new kinds of exploration. Imagine autonomous space probes capable of making discoveries without needing constant oversight or missions to exoplanets that adapt their trajectories based on real-time data. These possibilities are becoming less fiction and more reality with each passing day.

Furthermore, the integration of AI into space missions exemplifies a broader shift towards reliance on advanced technology to solve complex problems. It showcases how intertwined our scientific pursuits have become with machine learning and other emerging fields. As AI grows smarter and more capable, its contributions to space will undoubtedly inspire awe and ignite curiosity about what lies beyond our planetary doorstep.

Potential Breakthroughs in Quantum Computing

Imagine a world where computers can process information at lightning speed, solving the kind of complex problems that today's supercomputers struggle with. This could soon become reality thanks to the marriage of quantum computing and artificial intelligence (AI). When we talk about quantum computing, we're essentially talking about a whole new level of computational might, one that promises exponential boosts in processing power. Think of it as upgrading from a bicycle to a rocket ship. This leap means AI algorithms can tackle problems that were once considered impossible or far too time-consuming to solve.

So, how exactly does this increase in processing power change things for AI? At its core, AI relies on data and complex algorithms to make predictions, recognize patterns, and learn over time. With quantum computing, these processes could be supercharged; tasks that require immense computational effort, like modeling climate change or predicting stock market trends, could become more feasible. AI could also improve aspects of quantum algorithm development themselves, potentially unlocking new ways to secure communications via breakthroughs in cryptography or enhancing simulations of intricate systems, such as molecular structures or financial models.

One area that's particularly fascinating is cryptography. Currently, much of our online security depends on encryption techniques. These methods work under the assumption that it would take traditional computers an impractically long time to crack them. Quantum computers, due to their tremendous processing abilities, could potentially break these codes in hours or minutes. It's a double-edged sword: while this poses a threat to current security protocols, AI-driven advancements may help us stay ahead, developing even more sophisticated encryption methods to counteract potential threats.

However, it's not all smooth sailing in quantum land. One significant hurdle is dealing with quantum decoherence—a problem where quantum information loses its stability due to environmental interference. In simple terms, it's like trying to hear a whisper in a bustling room. Deciphering this digital noise is critical to ensure quantum computers operate effectively. AI might offer a solution here, with machine learning techniques playing a key role in designing better quantum architectures, optimizing them to mitigate the effects of decoherence and enhance robustness.

But what happens when we start applying this powerful collaboration between quantum computing and AI to real industries? The possibilities are mind-boggling. Take finance, for instance. The sheer volume of data and the complexity of market dynamics can overwhelm current systems. Quantum-enhanced AI could bring about unprecedented accuracy in predictive financial models, offering deeper insights into market trends. The same goes for healthcare, where the ability to quickly analyze extensive datasets could lead to breakthroughs in personalized medicine, allowing for treatments tailored to individuals' genetic profiles.

Logistics, too, stands to gain immensely. With AI's prowess in pattern recognition and prediction, combined with quantum computing's processing speed, complex systems like supply chains could see transformative efficiencies. Imagine significantly reduced delivery times, optimized resource allocations, and minimized costs—transformative changes brought about by smarter, faster data analysis.

While this future sounds promising, it's crucial to acknowledge the challenges and consider the broader implications of these technologies joining forces. As with any technological advancement, careful consideration of ethical, security, and societal impacts is essential. For instance, as quantum-enhanced AI systems begin to influence decision-making across various sectors, ensuring that these systems operate transparently and equitably becomes vital. We must strive to develop guidelines and frameworks that balance innovation with accountability and responsibility, fostering trust in AI-powered solutions.

Ethical AI Developments on the Horizon

In the ever-evolving world of artificial intelligence, discussions around ethics have taken center stage. As AI technologies advance, they bring potential benefits but also raise serious ethical questions that society must address. The increasing presence of AI in everyday life has prompted governments worldwide to draft legislation aimed at curbing its potential negative impacts, especially concerning user privacy and data protection. These legislative efforts are crucial as they lay down a framework that ensures transparency in AI operations, fostering trust between technology developers and users alike.

Governments are not working in isolation; they collaborate with various stakeholders, including academia, industry leaders, and civil society organizations. This broad-based approach is essential to creating comprehensive laws that encompass diverse perspectives and effectively safeguard public interests. By focusing on user privacy and data protection, these legislative measures aim to prevent misuse or unauthorized access to personal information, which could lead to harmful consequences if left unregulated. Transparency measures are equally important, as they ensure that AI systems operate in an understandable and predictable manner, allowing users to know exactly how their data is used and for what purposes.

Parallel to governmental actions, organizations within the tech industry are proactively establishing ethical guidelines to promote fairness and mitigate biases in AI systems. These guidelines often include principles that ensure algorithms do not unfairly discriminate against certain groups based on race, gender, or other demographic factors. Achieving fairness in AI requires constant vigilance and ongoing evaluation of how machine learning models are designed, trained, and deployed.

Furthermore, some organizations are advocating for the establishment of ethical certification standards for AI technologies. Such certifications could serve as a seal of approval, indicating that a particular AI system adheres to recognized ethical norms and practices. This not only reassures consumers but also incentivizes companies to adopt responsible practices in AI development. The creation and implementation of these guidelines require collaboration across sectors —including tech companies, regulators, and ethicists—to develop robust standards that align with societal values.

The conversation about AI ethics is not confined to policymakers and industry professionals alone. Increased awareness of ethical concerns surrounding AI has fueled public demand for responsible AI solutions. People are becoming more conscious of the implications of AI technologies and expect transparency and accountability from the companies that develop them. This growing public interest influences how media portrays AI, highlighting both its potential benefits and the need for careful consideration of its ethical impacts.

Media plays a pivotal role in shaping public perceptions by sharing stories that emphasize the importance of ethical considerations in technology development. By highlighting real-world scenarios where ethical AI applications have positively impacted society, media can help demystify AI and foster a more informed discourse. Conversely, it can also shed light on instances where lack of oversight or poor ethical standards have led to adverse effects, underscoring the necessity for rigorous ethical scrutiny in AI deployment.

As AI continues to expand into new territories, the collaboration between ethicists, policymakers, and technologists becomes increasingly critical. These collaborations are vital to ensuring that innovation does not outpace ethical responsibility. Ethicists bring valuable insight into the human and social implications of AI systems, while technologists offer expertise on technical possibilities and limitations. Policymakers bridge the gap by crafting regulations that uphold ethical principles without stifling technological progress.

For example, in healthcare, AI has the capacity to revolutionize patient diagnosis and treatment plans. However, without careful ethical considerations, there could be risks related to data privacy, informed consent, and even algorithmic bias. In this context, interdisciplinary collaboration ensures that AI innovations contribute positively to society while minimizing potential harm. Ethicists might advise on consent protocols, technologists could elucidate data requirements and security measures, while policymakers enact laws that protect patient rights.

Balancing innovation with responsibility is no small feat, yet it is imperative as AI's capabilities grow. Laws and ethical frameworks must evolve alongside technological advancements to remain relevant and effective. Continuous dialogue among all stakeholders fosters a shared understanding of the ethical landscape and encourages collective action toward sustainable development of AI technologies.

AI's Role in Tackling Climate Change

In the fight against climate change and for environmental sustainability, artificial intelligence (AI) is emerging as a powerful ally. One of the most significant contributions AI makes to this cause is through analyzing large environmental datasets. With an abundance of data gathered from satellites, sensors, and various monitoring systems around the globe, it's nearly impossible for humans to sift through all this information comprehensively. However, AI excels at finding patterns in this vast sea of data, providing valuable insights into changes in the atmosphere, ocean temperatures, ice caps, and more. By identifying these trends, AI helps us understand the impacts of climate change over time, enabling policymakers to address pressing issues with actionable strategies.

Beyond analysis, AI plays a pivotal role in optimizing energy distribution through smart grids. These are modern electricity networks that use digital technology to monitor and manage the transport of electricity from all generation sources to meet the varying electricity demands of end-users. AI brings efficiency to these grids by predicting energy consumption patterns, ensuring that electricity is distributed when and where it's needed the most. This optimization means less wastage and more effective integration of renewable energy sources like wind and solar power, which are essential for sustainable future energy supply. For instance, AI can forecast solar panel productivity based on weather data or adjust wind turbine output by predicting wind speeds, making renewable energy a more reliable part of our power mix.

Agriculture, another critical sector in environmental sustainability, benefits greatly from AI innovations. Precision agriculture involves using AI technologies to enhance farming by reducing chemical inputs and managing resources efficiently. With AI-powered tools, farmers can determine the precise amount of water, fertilizers, and pesticides needed, significantly minimizing waste and environmental impact. Furthermore, these tools provide farmers with real-time data and recommendations to make informed decisions about crop management and soil health. Automated farming practices driven by AI can even lead to the development of chemical-free farming techniques, promoting healthier ecosystems and food production methods.

Moreover, AI shows promise in predicting natural disasters, a crucial aspect of mitigating their catastrophic impacts. By processing climate and geological data, AI models can predict hurricanes, floods, wildfires, and more with increasing accuracy. This forecasting capability allows communities to prepare better and implement disaster response strategies proactively, ultimately saving lives and reducing economic loss. For example, AI models that predict floods can inform evacuation plans well in advance, while those that forecast wildfires can help allocate firefighting resources more effectively.

Enhancing climate models is yet another domain where AI shines. Traditional climate models, although advanced, have their limitations due to the complexity of the Earth's systems and the massive scale of computations required. AI enhances these models by improving their accuracy and speed, enabling scientists to simulate different climate scenarios more efficiently. This advancement aids in planning for future resource allocation by assessing potential outcomes of various environmental policies and interventions.

For AI to be a useful tool in combating climate change, understanding its guidelines in specific areas is beneficial. In optimizing energy use within smart grids, it's important to adopt AI systems that continuously learn from evolving energy patterns. This ensures they remain effective amidst changing demands and resource availability. Similarly, in supporting sustainable agriculture, implementing AI requires focusing on transparent data collection and system adaptability to local farming conditions. Farmers should receive training and support to seamlessly integrate AI technologies into their existing practices, maximizing benefits while maintaining ecological balance.

Disaster response practices enhanced by AI benefit significantly from collaboration among governments, NGOs, and tech companies. Each stakeholder can provide unique resources and expertise, ensuring AI solutions are robust, reliable, and widely accessible. In addition, integrating AI-enhanced climate models with global climate initiatives can contribute to a coordinated response against climate change challenges, fostering international cooperation and knowledge sharing.

Bringing It All Together

As we wrap up our exploration of AI's role across different domains, it's clear that artificial intelligence is not just a passing trend but a transformative force with far-reaching implications. From the roads we travel to the stars above, AI is reshaping how we interact with our environment and solve complex problems. We've seen how autonomous vehicles can reduce accidents and transform urban landscapes. Meanwhile, AI in space exploration offers new perspectives on our universe, enhancing our ability to gather and analyze data from afar. These advancements highlight the potential of AI to improve efficiency and safety in ways we never thought possible.

Looking into the future, the possibilities are as exciting as they are challenging. The integration of AI into quantum computing could unlock unprecedented processing power, changing the game in sectors like finance and healthcare. Ethical considerations remain crucial, ensuring that these powerful tools benefit society responsibly and equitably. AI's potential in tackling climate change shows promise, offering innovative solutions to enhance sustainability. As we continue this journey, staying informed and open-minded about AI's evolving role will be key. Remember, it's a tool meant to serve us, and with mindful application, it holds the promise of a better world.

Chapter 11

AI in Global Policy and Governance

A rtificial Intelligence (AI) is weaving its way into the fabric of global governance, presenting both opportunities and challenges for nations worldwide. As AI technologies evolve at a rapid pace, they find themselves crossing paths with existing international systems of management and oversight. This intersection is not merely technical; it has significant implications for how countries collaborate, create policies, and establish norms in an increasingly interconnected world. The integration of AI into global policy frameworks sparks a lively conversation about harmonizing technological advancement with ethical standards and cultural values. It's a topic that brings together policymakers, scholars, and tech enthusiasts to ponder the future direction of governance in the AI era.

In this chapter, we dive deep into how AI intersects with global governance structures, focusing on the development of international cooperation. Here's what's on the agenda: we'll explore the role of multilateral organizations like the United Nations in addressing AI standards and ethics. You'll read about how collaborative research initiatives can empower nations to develop standardized technologies that are compatible across borders. Plus, we'll touch upon the unique hurdles faced by developing countries and why inclusive dialogues are essential for fair AI governance. We'll also look at some successful case studies of international cooperation and discuss the importance of treaties and regulations in shaping AI's ethical and practical use. By the end of this chapter, you'll have a clearer understanding of how AI is reshaping the landscape of global policy and governance. Get ready to discover how countries can work together to ensure that AI benefits everyone while respecting each nation's unique context.

International Cooperation on AI Standards

In the evolving landscape of artificial intelligence (AI), establishing global standards has become a pressing need. As AI technologies advance, they intersect with international governance structures, making it essential to foster collaborative efforts across nations. Global governance frameworks, led by organizations like the United Nations (UN), play a pivotal role in addressing AI standards. By providing a platform where countries can come together to discuss, debate, and decide on these standards, the UN helps prevent potential misuse of AI technologies. It's not just about setting rules; it's about creating an environment where AI development is guided by shared values, ensuring that advancements benefit humanity as a whole.

Collaboration at the international level is crucial for the effective standardization of AI technologies. Research initiatives that focus on shared projects are a significant step toward this goal. When countries participate in joint research, they pool their resources, expertise, and insights, which leads to the creation of standardized technologies that multiple nations can adopt. Such collaborative initiatives not only ensure technological compatibility across borders but also help distribute the benefits of AI more equitably. For instance, when European countries work together on AI research, they create systems that are interoperable across the continent, enhancing the utility and safety of these technologies.

Multilateral organizations, such as the Organization for Economic Cooperation and Development (OECD), are instrumental in facilitating discussions on AI ethics. These organizations set benchmarks and guidelines that member states can follow, creating a common ground for ethical AI use. The OECD, for example, bring together experts from various fields to debate the ethical implications of AI and to develop guidelines that address these concerns comprehensively. This ensures that countries have a framework to guide their AI policies, helping them align with global standards while respecting national contexts.

Developing countries, however, face unique challenges in adopting and implementing these global AI standards. Many of these nations struggle with infrastructure limitations, lack of technical expertise, and financial constraints, leading to difficulties in keeping pace with AI advancements. Hence, it is vital for global discussions about AI to be inclusive, taking into account the perspectives and needs of developing countries. By involving these countries in conversations about AI governance, the international community can work towards solutions that are fair and applicable worldwide. Inclusivity also provides opportunities for knowledge transfer, enabling developing nations to leapfrog technological hurdles and better integrate AI into their economies.

Moreover, there is a growing awareness of the necessity for universal guidelines to curb the misuse of AI. While AI holds tremendous potential for good, unchecked development could lead to scenarios where AI is exploited for malicious purposes, such as surveillance or disinformation campaigns. Universal guidelines serve as a moral compass, ensuring that AI technologies are developed and used responsibly. They provide a framework for accountability, holding developers and users to international standards of conduct. Such guidelines are not just theoretical—they have practical implications that safeguard privacy, protect rights, and promote transparency in AI applications.

To illustrate the success of international cooperation in AI governance, several case studies highlight how countries have effectively worked together to manage AI's global impact. One notable instance is the partnership between Canada and France to establish the Global Partnership on Artificial Intelligence (GPAI). This initiative brings together experts from government, industry, and academia to collaborate on AI projects that uphold ethical principles. Through GPAI, participating countries share best practices and drive innovation while ensuring that AI developments align with societal values.

Treaties and regulations also play a crucial role in setting AI standards. They act as binding agreements that enforce adherence to agreed-upon norms and principles. Countries that sign these treaties commit to maintaining certain ethical standards in their AI practices. This commitment promotes trust among nations, fostering an environment where AI can thrive without compromising ethical integrity or security.

Regulating AI in Digital Economies

In today's fast-paced technological landscape, the intersection of artificial intelligence (AI) and global governance structures has become a focal point of conversation and legislation. As countries strive to harness AI's potential while ensuring its ethical use, crafting regulations that balance innovation and security is paramount. This journey begins with understanding how market regulations can be crafted to adapt businesses to new AI rules while simultaneously promoting responsible innovation.

Market regulations are critical because they set the playing field for how AI technologies are developed, tested, and deployed. They serve as a guide for businesses, enabling them to innovate within a framework that ensures safety and accountability. For instance, when a government imposes privacy laws specific to AI applications, companies must develop technologies that comply with these standards. It pushes firms toward innovations that prioritize consumer data protection, fostering trust between users and AI systems. This responsible approach not only builds public confidence but also encourages companies to innovate in ways that enhance both product quality and societal well-being.

Creating agile regulations is another crucial factor in maintaining a balance between fostering innovation and ensuring necessary safeguards. Agile regulations allow policies to be updated swiftly to keep pace with rapid advancements in AI technology. Traditional regulatory processes are often slow, which can stymie innovation. In contrast, flexible guidelines permit experimentation and growth while keeping a close eye on ethical considerations. An example of agility in action can be seen in sandbox environments where companies test AI solutions under regulatory oversight. These controlled settings allow for real-time policy adjustments based on outcomes, leading to smarter and more effective regulation over time.

Digital sovereignty emerges as another dynamic in this equation, with countries increasingly asserting control over their AI technologies. This assertion can have profound impacts on multinational companies. By setting local standards for AI usage and data management, nations aim to protect their citizens' data and preserve national interests. Such measures challenge multinational corporations to navigate varying regulations across borders. For example, the European Union's General Data Protection Regulation (GDPR) has set high standards for data privacy, influencing global companies to adjust their operations globally to comply. This type of digital sovereignty prompts companies to innovate not only technologically but also in their compliance strategies, ensuring they remain operational across diverse regulatory landscapes.

The economic impacts of AI regulations extend beyond compliance and innovation; they affect job markets and necessitate collaboration between policymakers and industry leaders. As AI continues to integrate into various sectors, there are concerns about job displacement due to automation. However, regulations can mitigate these effects by incentivizing companies to create roles that complement AI technology rather than replace human workers. Additionally, developing policies that support skills training programs helps the workforce transition smoothly into AI-enhanced roles.

Policymaker-industry collaboration is also vital in shaping effective AI regulations. When governments work with tech companies, academia, and industry stakeholders, they gain diverse perspectives that inform balanced policymaking. For instance, engaging with industry experts can provide insights into technological feasibility and implementation challenges, helping craft realistic and effective regulations. Similarly, involving academic researchers ensures the latest scientific findings guide policy decisions.

Governments must recognize the dual nature of AI's impact on economies — the opportunity for economic growth versus the potential for disruption. Countries that manage to strike the right balance can harness AI's growth in a way that stimulates economic prosperity. The development of robust AI ecosystems can lead to increased foreign investment, encouraging multinational companies to establish operations in regions that offer favorable regulatory environments. This influx of business activity creates jobs, boosts local economies, and enhances technological capabilities.

Finally, fostering an open dialogue between skeptics and advocates of AI plays a crucial role in shaping public sentiment and guiding ethical considerations in AI governance. Transparency in the regulatory process helps demystify AI technologies for the general populace, reducing fear and opposition. Public forums, workshops, and educational campaigns can be instrumental in achieving this transparency, providing a platform for diverse voices to express concerns and aspirations regarding AI development.

AI Policies within Various Nations

As we delve into the world of AI policies around the globe, it's essential to appreciate how different countries approach this transformative technology. A comparative analysis reveals that nations like the United States, China, and European Union members have distinct strategies that reflect their priorities and challenges. For instance, the United States focuses heavily on fostering innovation in AI with minimal regulations, driven by a culture that values freedom and entrepreneurship. Meanwhile, China adopts a more centralized approach, emphasizing state control and large-scale AI integration into societal infrastructure, which aligns with its overarching governance style. The European Union, on the other hand, prioritizes ethical considerations and data privacy, striving to set high standards for AI usage that align with its commitment to human rights and consumer protection.

These strategic differences are not arbitrary. They mirror each nation's broader political and cultural landscapes, as well as its economic goals. Similarities can also be found; many leading nations recognize the potential of AI to drive economic growth, improve efficiency, and enhance citizens' quality of life. Consequently, these countries invest heavily in research and development and collaborate with private sectors to accelerate AI deployment across various industries.

The path to defining effective AI policies is fraught with obstacles. Regulatory challenges arise from political, ethical, and economic arenas, each presenting unique hurdles. Politically, the rapid pace of AI advancements often outstrips legislative processes, leaving governments struggling to keep up with necessary regulatory frameworks. This discord creates gaps where AI applications might operate in legal gray areas, potentially leading to unintended consequences.

Ethical concerns loom large in discussions around AI policy. Ensuring AI systems are fair, accountable, and transparent is no small feat. Policymakers must grapple with questions about bias in AI algorithms, the right to privacy, and the moral implications of AI-driven decisions in critical sectors like healthcare and criminal justice. Balancing these ethical considerations with the need for technological progress requires nuanced understanding and robust dialogue between stakeholders.

Economically, there's the challenge of harmonizing AI policies with market demands. Striking a balance between encouraging innovation and protecting consumers necessitates agile and forward-thinking regulations that can adapt to technological changes without stifling creativity. Moreover, there's a global aspect to consider — divergent AI policies could lead to trade inefficiencies or conflicts among nations striving to protect intellectual property while promoting cross-border collaboration.

An often overlooked but crucial aspect of forming AI policies is citizen engagement. The integration of AI into everyday life has profound implications, touching on personal privacy, job dynamics, and social interactions. Therefore, it is vital for policymakers to involve citizens in discussions about the impacts of AI. Public consultations, town hall meetings, and educational campaigns can foster a shared understanding of AI's benefits and risks, ensuring that policy decisions align with societal values and expectations.

Citizen participation does more than democratize policymaking; it enriches it by incorporating diverse viewpoints and experiences, which can highlight practical challenges and opportunities that experts and technocrats might overlook. Engaged citizens can act as watchdogs, holding governments and corporations accountable for ethical AI use and advocating for transparency and fairness.

Lastly, interpreting AI policies is a dynamic process influenced by stakeholder perspectives. Stakeholders ranging from government agencies and tech companies to non-profits and academic institutions bring varied interests and insights into the mix. As technology evolves, so too must policies, adapting to new realities and challenges. For example, as AI becomes more integrated into sectors like transportation through autonomous vehicles, existing regulations around safety and liability require reevaluation and, possibly, extensive overhaul.

Stakeholder influence extends beyond shaping policy; they play a pivotal role in policy evolution. Tech companies may lobby for regulations that favor innovation speed, while advocacy groups might prioritize ethical safeguards. Balancing these interests ensures that AI advances are aligned with both economic incentives and societal well-being.

AI's Influence on Cybersecurity Agendas

In the fast-evolving world of global cybersecurity, AI is playing a pivotal role in transforming how we handle digital threats. Gone are the days when security measures relied solely on manual monitoring and simple software systems. Today, AI enhances our defenses by revolutionizing threat detection systems. This transformation is largely due to machine learning models that quickly identify patterns and anomalies. These advanced systems can detect cyber threats far more efficiently than traditional methods, offering an invaluable edge in safeguarding digital infrastructures.

AI-driven threat intelligence is taking this a step further by using precise algorithms for real-time threat identification and assessment. Imagine algorithms capable of analyzing vast amounts of data to pinpoint unusual activities. For example, AI systems can flag suspicious login attempts or unauthorized access to secure networks instantaneously. This level of threat intelligence streamlines responses and significantly reduces the window of opportunity for malicious actors. As a result, organizations can swiftly adapt their security strategies, staying one step ahead of potential breaches.

However, with great power comes great responsibility. The same tools that bolster security can also be misused, raising ethical concerns that cannot be overlooked. The misuse of AI in cybersecurity presents risks such as privacy invasion, widespread surveillance, and the deployment of autonomous hacking systems. These concerns demand comprehensive countermeasures to prevent potential abuses. Ethical considerations must inform the development and deployment of AI technologies, ensuring they serve collective interests without compromising individual rights.

International cooperation is crucial in fortifying these efforts. With cyber threats transcending borders, countries must collaborate extensively to safeguard against increasingly sophisticated attacks. This collaboration manifests through shared intelligence, joint task forces, and standardized practices that unite nations in their fight against cybercrime. By pooling resources and expertise, countries are better equipped to respond to incidents swiftly and effectively, reinforcing a collective cybersecurity posture.

For instance, international organizations like INTERPOL and the European Union Agency for Cybersecurity (ENISA) facilitate information sharing and coordinated responses between countries. These collaborations help create a unified front against cybercriminals who exploit jurisdictional vulnerabilities. Additionally, frameworks like the Budapest Convention on Cybercrime provide legal standards that guide international cooperation, promoting consistency and accountability across borders.

The integration of AI in cybersecurity not only fortifies defense mechanisms but also necessitates a reevaluation of ethical guidelines to manage its potential misuse. Organizations and governments must consider the implications of AI-driven surveillance and ensure robust oversight mechanisms are in place. By doing so, they can mitigate risks while leveraging AI's capabilities to strengthen global security frameworks.

As AI continues to evolve, its potential to reshape global cybersecurity strategies will likely expand. Businesses, governments, and individuals all stand to benefit from improved security measures if we responsibly harness the power of AI. However, vigilance remains key to ensuring that AI is a force for good—one that protects rather than endangers. By embracing innovation while upholding ethical standards, we pave the way for safer digital environments across the globe.

The Impact of AI on International Relations

The influence of AI on global diplomatic relationships and power dynamics is profound, with nations now harnessing this technology to gain a geopolitical edge. Strategic competition in international politics increasingly involves leveraging AI capabilities, with countries vying to surpass one another in AI innovation and application. This pursuit is not just about who has the best technology; it directly affects national security. For instance, AI can enhance intelligence operations, cybersecurity measures, and defense systems, giving technologically advanced nations a significant advantage over others. Consequently, countries that lag behind in AI development might find themselves vulnerable or at a disadvantage in global negotiations.

In recent years, we've observed how AI-driven policies have begun to shape diplomatic relations. Trade negotiations are one area where this change is visible. When nations integrate AI technologies into their economies, they often reassess existing trade terms to align with new capabilities and limitations. This can lead to shifts in longstanding trade partnerships or the establishment of new ones based on mutual technological interests. Furthermore, AI facilitates improved communication channels between countries. Advanced AI algorithms can analyze vast amounts of data to identify trends and predict outcomes in ways humans cannot, allowing diplomats to make more informed decisions during negotiations. These technological advancements could potentially break down barriers, leading to improved understanding and collaboration between nations.

However, this evolving dynamic also presents risks, as AI's role in global governance could alter power balances and influence treaties and international stability. As AI becomes integrated into decision-making processes, the potential for manipulation and bias increases. Powerful AI systems could be used to sway political opinions or even destabilize governments through misinformation campaigns. Additionally, the disparity in AI capabilities between developed and developing nations could exacerbate existing inequalities, impacting how treaties are negotiated and enforced. The risk is that only those nations with robust AI infrastructures will have significant say in international agreements, marginalizing less technologically-advanced countries.

Public perception of AI plays a crucial role in shaping national narratives and influencing international relations. Media portrayal heavily guides these perceptions by highlighting either the benefits or threats associated with AI developments. Positive media coverage can foster acceptance and enthusiasm toward AI-driven advancements, bolstering national interest and investment in the field. Conversely, fear-based narratives may lead to public resistance against AI adoption, affecting how a nation approaches its AI strategies on the global stage. For example, if a country's citizens believe AI poses significant risks to jobs or privacy, this sentiment could drive policy decisions that restrict its integration, impacting international cooperative efforts around AI.

It's essential to recognize that while some aspects of AI's influence on diplomacy are currently visible, many potential impacts remain speculative because the technology itself is rapidly evolving. Despite this uncertainty, what is clear is that nations must navigate this terrain carefully, balancing the opportunities presented by AI with the ethical and practical challenges it brings. As AI continues to infiltrate various facets of global governance, the importance of establishing common ground and frameworks for cooperation cannot be overstated. Diplomatic efforts should focus on fostering dialogue and collaboration among nations to mitigate risks and maximize the positive impacts of AI on global stability and progress.

While strategic competition and diplomatic relations reflect immediate impacts of AI, the broader implications for governance structures require ongoing assessment and adaptation. Nations must keep pace with technological advancements and continuously evaluate how these changes affect international relations. In doing so, countries can work collectively towards a future where AI serves as a tool for progress and peace rather than division and conflict.

Insights and Implications

In this chapter, we've explored how international cooperation plays a pivotal role in shaping AI standards and governance. By working together through organizations like the UN and OECD, countries can pool resources and set ethical guidelines that ensure AI development benefits everyone. It's clear that collaboration is key—countries sharing research and expertise make it easier to create standardized, fair, and interoperable AI technologies across borders. This teamwork not only boosts innovation but also levels the playing field for developing nations, helping them overcome unique challenges and integrate AI into their economies effectively.

We've also touched on the need for universal guidelines to prevent AI misuse. While AI offers incredible possibilities, it's crucial to have rules in place to avoid scenarios where technology becomes harmful. These global standards serve as a moral guide, ensuring that AI is developed responsibly and transparently. The success stories of partnerships like those between Canada and France show us that when countries unite under shared values, they can manage AI's global impact positively. As we move forward, these cooperative efforts will be vital in navigating AI's complex relationship with global governance.

Chapter 12

Cultivating AI Literacy

C ultivating AI literacy is all about understanding and embracing the world of artificial intelligence. It's not just for tech wizards— anyone can dive in and start learning. The digital age we live in is filled with AI-powered gadgets, from smart assistants to personalized recommendations on streaming services. Yet, many people are hesitant or unsure about how AI works and what it means for their lives. This chapter sheds light on how we can become more familiar with AI, offering a welcoming hand to those eager to learn but not sure where to begin. With AI becoming more embedded in our daily routines, understanding its nuances doesn't need to be overwhelming. It's like meeting a new friend; the more you know, the less mysterious it becomes.

This chapter offers readers a guide on how to boost their understanding of AI through various practical steps. It delves into integrating AI education into schools and highlights the importance of teacher training. You'll also find insights into community-based learning initiatives that make concepts accessible to everyone. Plus, there's a focus on resources that encourage self-learning, so individuals can explore AI at their own pace. The chapter emphasizes open discussions about AI's impacts and ethical considerations, encouraging a balanced view on technology's role in society. By weaving these educational elements together, the goal is to create a well-informed public that can confidently navigate an AI-driven future.

Integration of AI Education in Schools

Introducing AI concepts into educational curricula is crucial in preparing students for a future increasingly shaped by technology. By tailoring curriculum development to different age groups, we can establish a foundational understanding of AI early on while minimizing the apprehension it might initially provoke. Younger students could engage with simple AI concepts through interactive games and storytelling that illustrate how AI touches everyday life, such as recommending songs or providing directions. As they grow, students can delve deeper into the mechanics behind these familiar technologies, learning about algorithms or machine learning through relatable examples. This gradual progression demystifies AI, making it less intimidating and more accessible.

Proper training for educators plays a vital role in this effort. Teachers are on the frontline of student engagement and must be equipped with both knowledge and confidence to effectively convey complex AI topics. This involves professional development programs that not only educate teachers about AI but also guide them in crafting engaging lessons. For instance, workshops can offer hands-on experiences with AI tools, illustrating how AI functions in real-world scenarios. When educators feel assured in their ability to teach AI, they can nurture a spirit of curiosity among students, encouraging questions and exploration. This open environment has a profound impact on learning outcomes, as students are more likely to retain information when actively interested and involved in the subject matter.

Incorporating AI education through an interdisciplinary approach further enriches student understanding. By weaving AI concepts into subjects like math, science, and ethics, we can provide a more comprehensive view of its applications and implications. Imagine a math class where statistics and probability lessons include AI-related data sets, allowing students to visualize data analysis in action. In science classes, AI might be examined in the context of problem-solving experiments, such as predicting weather patterns or identifying species from photographs. Ethics discussions can tackle the moral and societal questions that arise from AI advancements, prompting students to reflect on bias, privacy, and decision-making. Ultimately, this holistic approach prepares students for diverse career paths, fostering a well-rounded worldview essential in today's job market.

Hands-on, project-based learning presents another valuable strategy in teaching AI. Through active participation in projects, students develop critical thinking and teamwork skills. For example, a classroom project might involve building simple AI models using block programming tools, which allow students to focus on developing logic without delving too deeply into coding syntax. Schools can facilitate hackathons or collaborative challenges where teams solve problems using AI principles, such as creating apps for local community issues. These projects encourage students to apply what they've learned practically, solidifying their understanding and sparking enthusiasm for innovation.

Guidelines become pivotal in structuring these educational initiatives. In curriculum development, it's crucial to design age-appropriate content that builds on prior knowledge, ensuring each student grasps fundamental concepts before advancing. Establishing clear objectives for what students should achieve at various stages can help maintain consistency and continuity across grade levels. Similarly, guidelines for teacher training programs should emphasize the importance of familiarizing educators with AI tools and resources so they can confidently guide students through the intricacies of AI technologies. Providing ongoing support and feedback mechanisms enables teachers to continually refine their methods and materials.

Project-based learning benefits from structured guidelines as well. By setting goals for each phase of a project, students remain focused on learning outcomes rather than losing direction amidst technological complexities. Clear instructions on collaboration, project timelines, and expected deliverables ensure a smooth process that keeps students engaged and accountable. This framework empowers students to manage their work effectively, emphasizing the value of shared responsibility and communication within teams.

Community-based AI Learning Initiatives

Engaging communities in learning about artificial intelligence (AI) is a crucial step towards building an informed society. To achieve this, various initiatives can be implemented to create environments where people of diverse backgrounds and expertise can gather, learn, and discuss AI-related topics. One effective method is through local workshops at community centers. These workshops are designed specifically to cater to adults who might possess limited technical knowledge but have a growing curiosity about AI. By focusing on everyday applications of AI, such as virtual assistants or online shopping algorithms, these sessions make complex concepts accessible and relatable. Furthermore, they encourage active participation by including interactive components like live demonstrations and hands-on activities.

Community centers are ideal locations for these workshops because they are approachable and often central in neighborhoods. They provide a non-intimidating setting where individuals can come together, ask questions, and learn without feeling overwhelmed. For example, a workshop could include a session on how AI impacts job markets, encouraging participants to consider how their own careers might evolve alongside technological advancements. This personalized approach helps demystify AI, making it less of an abstract concept and more of a tangible part of everyday life.

In addition to standalone efforts at the local level, partnerships with tech organizations play a significant role in spreading AI literacy. These collaborations can bring cutting-edge resources and expert knowledge into the community. Tech companies may supply guest speakers who can offer insights into the latest developments and trends in AI technology. Such exchanges not only enrich the learning experience but also draw in a wider audience who might otherwise feel disconnected from the tech industry's rapid pace. A key aspect of these partnerships is the mutual benefit: tech organizations gain valuable feedback from the community while participants acquire up-to-date information and networks that could support personal or professional growth.

A successful partnership should aim to bridge gaps between theory and practice. For instance, a local tech firm might work with a library or school to run a series of mini-projects where participants get to experiment with coding simple AI programs. This hands-on exposure is essential in drawing practitioners from diverse fields into the fold, showing them how AI tools can improve efficiencies or inspire new innovations in their industries.

Online communities and forums further enhance opportunities for AI learning by overcoming geographic barriers. These digital spaces allow individuals from around the world to connect, share experiences, and engage in stimulating discussions about AI's impact on modern living. The beauty of online forums lies in their accessibility; anyone with an internet connection can join conversations, ask questions, or access shared materials like articles, videos, and tutorials. Platforms like Reddit and Stack Exchange have vibrant AI subgroups where beginners can seek advice and experts can debate nuanced issues.

This global reach is particularly beneficial for those who live in areas where physical workshops or tech partnerships are not readily available. For instance, someone living in a rural area without easy access to a community center could still participate in an online webinar or join a virtual study group focused on AI ethics. Moreover, these forums facilitate continuous education, providing updates on the latest research findings or emerging technologies which can be quickly disseminated amongst members.

Public libraries, long-standing bastions of community knowledge, continue to evolve in their educational roles by hosting AI events and offering relevant materials. Libraries are uniquely positioned to serve as accessible venues for AI literacy projects due to their welcoming atmospheres and commitment to lifelong learning. They can host talks, workshops, or reading groups that focus on different aspects of AI, appealing to both novices and enthusiasts alike. For instance, a library might organize a series of lectures exploring AI's influence on privacy, guiding attendees in critical thinking about data security and surveillance.

Moreover, libraries can support AI initiatives by curating extensive collections of resources – from beginner-friendly books and articles to advanced academic papers and case studies. Libraries might partner with local colleges or universities to broaden their resource base, ensuring patrons have access to current, high-quality information. Through these offerings, libraries help dispel myths surrounding AI, providing facts and context that foster informed opinions among community members.

Resources for Self-learning AI Concepts

In today's fast-paced world, understanding artificial intelligence (AI) is more crucial than ever. For those eager to dive into this fascinating subject on their own terms and at their own pace, there are numerous resources available that cater to various learning styles and preferences.

A fantastic starting point for independent learners is online courses offered by platforms like Coursera, edX, and Udacity. These platforms provide an array of AI-focused courses that range from introductory to advanced levels. One key advantage they offer is flexibility, allowing learners to set their schedules and progress at a comfortable pace. This is particularly appealing to busy professionals or those with unpredictable daily routines. Moreover, many of these courses incorporate hands-on projects and real-world applications, enabling learners to develop tangible skills as they progress. Engaging in these projects helps demystify complex concepts through practical application, reinforcing theoretical knowledge with concrete experience.

While online courses stand out for their structured learning paths, books and podcasts present another valuable avenue for digging deeper into AI topics. Books offer comprehensive insights, often exploring the history, development, and implications of AI in society. They provide readers with the opportunity to engage critically with the content, encouraging them to question and reflect on what's being presented. On the other hand, podcasts bring these discussions to life through engaging storytelling. Listening to experts debate, discuss, and dissect various AI topics can spark curiosity and foster a deeper understanding. For instance, some podcasts delve into ethical considerations, while others may focus on technological advancements or societal impacts. The narrative style of podcasts makes them enjoyable for auditory learners and ideal for multitasking during commutes or workouts.

For those who learn visually, educational YouTube channels are a treasure trove of resources simplifying complex AI ideas. Channels such as Computerphile, Two Minute Papers, and CrashCourse break down intricate subjects using visual content and animations, making the material more digestible. They also frequently feature real-life applications, showcasing how AI influences everyday life and driving home its relevance. Watching these videos not only aids comprehension but also keeps viewers engaged, making it easier to grasp challenging concepts without feeling overwhelmed.

Another exciting option for lifelong learners interested in AI is experimenting with tools like Google Colab. As an AI experimentation lab, Google Colab allows users to write and execute Python code over the cloud, removing the need for high-powered personal hardware. This accessibility makes it easier for beginners to experiment without the typical barriers associated with coding environments. By diving into hands-on coding experiments, learners can gain firsthand experience in training models, manipulating datasets, and understanding algorithms. This experiential approach fosters a more intimate understanding of AI processes, offering opportunities to apply theoretical knowledge practically.

These various resources collectively cater to diverse learning preferences—whether one prefers reading, listening, watching, or doing —and empower individuals to explore AI independently. However, given the broad and often technical nature of AI, it's important to establish a guideline when approaching online courses to maximize their educational benefit. Start by identifying your goals: Are you seeking a basic understanding, or do you wish to specialize in a particular area, like machine learning or neural networks? Understanding your objectives will help you select the right course. Furthermore, engage with community forums related to your course, as discussing topics with peers can reinforce learning and provide support.

Promoting Open Discussions About AI Impacts

Understanding AI and its implications is a journey that calls for open dialogues and shared knowledge. Engaging discussions about technology, such as those found in public forums and panels, play a crucial role in demystifying AI's societal impact. These gatherings are not just about experts touting complex ideas; they're valuable opportunities for experts, enthusiasts, skeptics, and laypeople to come together under one roof. By inviting a mix of voices—scientists, technologists, ethicists, and everyday citizens—these panels balance optimistic visions of AI with the necessary skepticism. For example, while a tech developer might highlight advancements in AI medical diagnostics, a privacy advocate can raise concerns about data security. Such balanced exchanges prevent bias and help attendees form nuanced perspectives.

Moreover, an inclusive dialogue at these forums encourages critical thinking among participants. When people hear different viewpoints and engage in healthy debates, it stimulates them to think deeper about AI and its broader implications. Questions like "How will AI change our jobs?" or "What ethical boundaries should guide AI development?" might surface, prompting further exploration and community learning. Guidelines on how to conduct these forums effectively can lead to productive outcomes, ensuring that discussions remain accessible and engaging for everyone involved.

Moving beyond traditional settings, social media has emerged as a powerful platform to democratize conversations about AI. Campaigns on platforms like Twitter, Instagram, and TikTok break down barriers between those who are tech-savvy and those who aren't. Through interactive posts, live Q&A sessions, and direct messages, these campaigns reach a larger audience, sparking interest and engagement among individuals who might otherwise feel alienated from technical discussions. For instance, a viral hashtag campaign that invites users to share their thoughts on AI in daily life can generate diverse inputs, expanding the conversation beyond expert circles.

On social media, the simplified language and real-time interactions make it easier for people to voice their opinions and learn from others. Technology novices often find comfort in discovering they're not alone in their questions or doubts about AI. This shared learning experience breaks down intimidation factors, fostering a more approachable entry into AI literacy.

Community events serve as yet another platform to foster public understanding, particularly focusing on the ethical implications of AI. These events often take the form of workshops or fairs, where residents can engage through hands-on activities and thought-provoking dialogues. Interactive stations might simulate AI decision-making processes, allowing participants to see firsthand how machines interpret data and make choices. Such tangible exercises encourage attendees to consider the moral dimensions of AI and discuss potential consequences with their peers.

In community settings, hosting discussions around scenarios like AI in policing or healthcare provides a framework for visitors to debate ethics grounded in reality. Organizers may pose questions: "Should AI have the final say in medical diagnoses?" or "How does AI-driven surveillance impact privacy rights?" These inquiries provoke reflection and discourse, urging communities to weigh AI benefits against possible ethical quandaries. Providing guidelines on effectively running these events—by setting objectives and clear discussion flow—can enhance participation and depth of inquiry.

Collaborations between schools and businesses offer another avenue to bridge educational gaps related to AI. These partnerships create pathways for students and professionals to gain firsthand insights and apply classroom learning to real-world contexts. For example, businesses might host internship programs where students participate in AI projects, seeing theory come to life. Companies can also deliver guest lectures or workshops at schools, sharing current industry trends and challenges.

By aligning educational goals with business needs, these collaborations prepare learners for future job markets increasingly shaped by AI. Schools benefit from cutting-edge knowledge and practical resources, while businesses groom a new generation of talent equipped to tackle evolving technological landscapes. It's crucial for educators and companies to share best practices on structuring these partnerships to ensure mutually beneficial outcomes. This includes defining clear objectives, maintaining regular communication, and establishing benchmarks for evaluation.

Building an Informed Public on AI Ethics

Understanding the ethical considerations of artificial intelligence (AI) is increasingly becoming a necessity for everyone. AI impacts nearly every aspect of our lives, from how we communicate and work to the way we make critical decisions. Yet, for those who aren't steeped in technology's complex world, understanding these effects can be daunting. This is where educational outreach through seminars becomes invaluable. By providing structured yet engaging sessions, educators help demystify AI ethics and promote the responsible use of technology.

Let's consider the power of seminars. They offer an opportunity to explain AI ethics in a relatable manner, breaking down intricate ideas into understandable concepts. Such events bring people together, fostering a shared learning experience. Through these gatherings, individuals can ask questions and engage in discussions that might otherwise seem intimidating. Imagine attending an AI ethics seminar where experts present case studies on how AI affects privacy or job displacement. You begin to see the real-world implications, moving beyond abstract theories to grasp tangible realities.

Now, delve deeper into such case studies. These are like windows into AI's true nature, showcasing its benefits and potential pitfalls. For instance, look at facial recognition technology. While it offers advancements in security and law enforcement, it also raises serious ethical concerns about privacy and surveillance. By analyzing cases where AI was used ethically and where it wasn't, learners develop critical thinking skills. They start asking essential questions like, "What values should guide AI development?" or "How do we ensure AI is fair and unbiased?"

To further nurture understanding, developing resources that simplify ethical frameworks is crucial. Creating accessible materials means transforming complex information into digestible content. Think of guides, pamphlets, or online resources that break down AI ethics into everyday language. People shouldn't have to be experts to understand what AI is doing behind the scenes. These resources empower communities by making ethical questions approachable, equipping them with the tools needed for informed discussion.

Consider an example where a community center introduces a workbook titled "AI Ethics Made Simple." It walks readers through basic principles, offering scenarios and diagrams illustrating key points. Suddenly, AI ethics isn't just a niche topic but something accessible and relevant. When communities have access to such materials, they become equipped to voice their concerns and insights on how AI technologies intersect with their lives.

Furthermore, engaging stakeholders in meaningful collaborations can create pathways for substantial progress. Stakeholders include policymakers, tech companies, ethicists, and community leaders, all bringing diverse perspectives to the table. When these groups come together, they can hammer out guidelines ensuring AI aligns with societal values. Picture a roundtable discussion where representatives from various sectors debate AI's role in social media bias. By sharing expertise, they craft policies promoting transparency and accountability.

Such collaborations don't just produce documents; they foster a culture of inclusivity where all voices contribute to shaping AI's future. Society becomes a part of the conversation, not simply passive recipients of technological change. By including stakeholders in the process, we build trust and encourage adherence to ethical practices across industries.

Guidelines play a pivotal role here. Clearly articulated standards provide a roadmap for developers and users alike. They let everyone know what's acceptable and what isn't. Importantly, these guidelines aren't set in stone; they evolve as our understanding grows. Involving varied groups in their creation ensures they reflect broad perspectives, not narrow interests.

In this growing field, ethics cannot be an afterthought. To cultivate AI literacy effectively, the public needs active engagement and clear communication. Educational outreach lays the groundwork, sparking interest and understanding. Case studies animate the issues, turning theoretical debates into practical discussions. Resource development strips away complexities, empowering individuals to participate fully. Engaging stakeholders solidifies these efforts, creating a cohesive framework guiding AI's ethical trajectory.

As we look to the future, fostering an understanding of ethical considerations in AI usage among the general public becomes increasingly imperative. Technology continues to embed itself within our daily experiences, shaping decisions large and small. By prioritizing ethical literacy, we equip society with knowledge and foresight, preparing us to navigate AI's challenges and opportunities responsibly.

Summary and Reflections

Throughout this chapter, we've explored several strategies aimed at boosting public understanding of AI. We've delved into the importance of integrating AI education into schools and how community-based initiatives can foster AI literacy among diverse groups. From combining AI with various school subjects to hosting workshops in community centers, these efforts are all about making AI relatable and less intimidating. This chapter also highlights the role of both traditional methods and online forums in spreading AI knowledge, offering plenty of ways for anyone curious about AI to engage and learn.

In addition, we touched on the vital aspect of promoting open discussions around AI's societal impacts and ethical considerations. We discussed how seminars, social media, and community events can provide accessible platforms for dialogues that involve everyone, not just tech specialists. These conversations are crucial because they help demystify AI, encouraging critical thinking and balanced views. By weaving educational outreach and engaging stakeholders, we're building a society that's not only informed but ready to navigate AI's challenges and opportunities responsibly.

Chapter 13

Use Cases of AI Innovation

E xploring the use cases of AI innovation takes us into a world where technology is transforming everyday life in fascinating ways. From healthcare and city planning to agriculture and disaster response, AI is not just a concept of the future—it's a driving force actively shaping our present. Imagine having a personal health assistant that predicts potential medical issues before they arise or a virtual traffic cop managing congestion in your city. These are not just ideas but real-world applications already making tangible impacts across various sectors.

In this chapter, we'll delve into these revolutionary uses of AI with engaging examples that show exactly how it's helping solve complex global challenges. You'll see how AI helps doctors predict health risks, manage patient interactions, and even speed up drug discovery, leading to better healthcare outcomes. We'll also explore how smart cities are using AI for efficient traffic management and sustainable energy solutions, while agricultural practices benefit from precision farming and supply chain optimization. Plus, discover how AI strengthens disaster response capabilities and conservation efforts. By the end, you'll have a clearer understanding of AI's transformative role and be inspired by its potential to enhance our world on many levels.

AI in Personalized Healthcare Solutions

Artificial intelligence (AI) is increasingly influencing various sectors, and healthcare is no exception. It's transforming how medical professionals operate, offering more tailored patient care, and improving outcomes significantly. One impressive innovation in this field is predictive analytics. Imagine being able to foresee possible health risks before they become significant issues. Predictive analytics does precisely that by analyzing vast amounts of data from a patient's history, genetics, and even lifestyle choices. By doing so, it helps doctors anticipate potential health concerns, such as the risk of developing diabetes or heart disease. This foresight allows healthcare providers to implement preventive measures, like lifestyle changes or medication, long before any symptoms arise. These forward-thinking strategies not only improve patient health but can also dramatically cut down on healthcare costs by addressing issues early.

Another area where AI is making waves is patient interaction through chatbots. Hospitals and clinics often grapple with administrative burdens, which can detract from focusing on providing quality care. Enter AI-powered chatbots. These digital assistants manage routine inquiries from patients, such as appointment scheduling, symptom checks, or medication refill reminders. By handling these tasks, chatbots free up medical staff to concentrate on more critical aspects of patient care. Furthermore, they provide quick responses to patients' questions, enhancing overall satisfaction and engagement. It's a win-win situation where efficiency and patient-centered care both see improvements.

In drug discovery and development, AI offers groundbreaking advantages. Developing new medications traditionally takes years and involves high costs. However, AI has a knack for streamlining this process. Through machine learning algorithms, AI can analyze complex biological data to predict how potential drugs will react within the body. This capability is crucial in identifying and dismissing compounds likely to cause adverse effects. As a result, the drug development process becomes faster and more efficient, ultimately speeding up the availability of life-saving treatments to patients worldwide. Although drug discovery may seem removed from direct patient interaction, it's crucial to recognize its vital role in ensuring that those interactions lead to better outcomes through effective treatments.

Telehealth services have gained immense popularity, especially in recent times, and AI is a key player in their evolution. Managing chronic diseases such as hypertension, diabetes, or asthma can be challenging for patients and healthcare providers alike. AI-powered telehealth solutions provide an excellent platform for continuous monitoring and management of these conditions. With AI, telehealth systems can analyze data from wearable devices, track vital signs, and detect anomalies that might indicate health deterioration. Physicians can then adjust treatment plans remotely, ensuring prompt intervention without needing frequent in-person visits. For patients, this means more accessible and comprehensive care, tailored to their specific needs, from the comfort of their homes.

Moreover, AI in telehealth ensures personalized advice and support, automating alerts for medication schedules or important health check-ins. This ongoing care loop fosters proactive health management, reducing hospital readmissions and improving long-term health outcomes for patients with chronic illnesses. The convenience and accessibility provided by AI-driven telehealth solutions make them invaluable tools in modern healthcare.

Guidance plays a crucial role in maximizing these technologies. For instance, when it comes to predictive analytics in patient care, there should be a clear framework for how data is collected and utilized to ensure privacy and accuracy. Establishing ethical guidelines is essential to maintaining trust between patients and healthcare providers while harnessing the power of AI. Similarly, while deploying chatbots for patient interaction, it's vital to establish protocols on when human intervention is necessary, ensuring patients feel heard and their concerns addressed appropriately.

As we navigate this tech-driven transformation, it's important to remain open about both the benefits and challenges associated with AI in healthcare. For many, adapting to these changes requires understanding their implications and having confidence in their potential to enhance patient care. By implementing well-considered guidelines and embracing these advancements, AI stands poised to revolutionize healthcare and set new standards for patient-focused solutions globally.

Smart Cities Enhanced by AI Infrastructure

In the dynamic landscape of urban living, AI has emerged as a game-changer, transforming how cities operate and enhancing the quality of life for their inhabitants. Let's dive into some fascinating ways AI is reshaping urban management, starting with traffic systems.

Imagine driving through a bustling city without constantly hitting bottlenecks or getting stuck in seemingly endless traffic jams. This is becoming a reality thanks to AI-powered traffic management systems. These systems analyze vast amounts of data from cameras, GPS devices, and sensors to understand traffic patterns and predict congestion before it happens. Cities like Los Angeles have adopted such technologies to synchronize traffic lights, reducing stop-and-go traffic and improving the overall flow. What's more, by collecting real-time data, these systems can swiftly respond to accidents or road closures, rerouting vehicles and minimizing disruptions. As a guideline, when setting up AI traffic systems, integrating data from multiple sources ensures a comprehensive view of the traffic landscape, maximizing efficiency and safety.

Shifting gears towards energy management, AI is playing a crucial role in making cities more sustainable and economically efficient. By analyzing consumption patterns, AI-driven solutions can optimize energy distribution, ensuring that electricity is used where it's needed most while avoiding wastage. For example, AI can predict peak usage times and adjust power supply accordingly, reducing the risk of blackouts and lowering operational costs. In cities such as Amsterdam, smart grids powered by AI manage energy use dynamically, balancing supply and demand in real time. A useful guideline here is to focus on predictive analytics and flexible grid integration to maximize cost savings and minimize outages, ultimately fostering a more resilient urban environment.

Public safety is another critical area where AI is making significant strides, particularly through surveillance innovations. Traditional surveillance systems often require manual monitoring, which can be both time-consuming and prone to human error. Enter AI, which enhances these systems by automatically identifying unusual activity or security threats in real time. For instance, AI algorithms can flag suspicious behavior in public spaces, enabling authorities to respond promptly and effectively, thus preventing potential crimes. In Chicago, police departments are already leveraging AI to anticipate crime hotspots, deploying officers strategically to deter criminal activity. When implementing AI surveillance, it's important to establish clear privacy guidelines and involve community stakeholders to address concerns related to civil liberties and transparency.

Lastly, let's explore how AI is revolutionizing waste management. Efficient waste management is crucial for maintaining clean and healthy urban environments. AI-driven waste solutions not only streamline operations but also promote recycling efforts. By utilizing smart bins equipped with sensors, AI can monitor fill levels and optimize collection routes, ensuring that resources are used efficiently. Additionally, machine learning models can sort recyclables more accurately than manual methods, increasing recycling rates and reducing landfill waste. San Francisco's waste management system serves as a model, leveraging AI to achieve significant reductions in waste sent to landfills. Guidelines for successful integration include investing in adaptive learning systems that improve over time and fostering partnerships between technology providers and municipal authorities to tailor solutions to local needs.

AI-Driven Disaster Response Systems

When disaster strikes, response time and preparedness can mean the difference between chaos and control. AI plays a transformative role in enhancing disaster response strategies, beginning with predictive modeling. This innovation allows experts to analyze vast amounts of data to foresee disasters before they occur, enabling pre-emptive action. By examining patterns in weather data, geological activity, and historical events, AI can predict natural disasters more accurately than ever before. For instance, machine learning algorithms can identify subtle indicators of potential earthquakes or hurricanes, giving communities crucial lead time to brace for impact. This foresight minimizes damage by helping to inform risk mitigation plans, such as reinforcing infrastructure or optimizing evacuation protocols.

Another critical application of AI in disaster response lies in real-time resource allocation. During emergencies, efficient deployment of resources—such as medical supplies, rescue teams, and essential utilities—is paramount. AI systems can process incoming data from multiple sources, like satellite imagery and ground reports, to prioritize areas of greatest need. For example, during wildfires or floods, AI can pinpoint affected zones and suggest the optimal routes for delivering aid, reducing delays caused by human error or outdated maps. This smart allocation ensures that emergency services are not only swift but also precisely targeted, maximizing their impact.

Equally important is the role of AI in keeping people informed through enhanced communication systems. In times of crisis, accurate and timely information is vital for public safety. AI-powered platforms can filter and disseminate information across various channels—social media, news broadcasts, and mobile alerts. By analyzing social networks and other data streams, AI detects emerging situations, verifies facts, and updates authorities and the public in real-time. For instance, during a hurricane, AI can assess live data to provide updates on storm paths, shelter availability, and traffic conditions. This widespread communication can prevent panic, direct people to safety, and coordinate efforts among different agencies.

Post-disaster, AI also contributes significantly to recovery analysis and planning. After the initial emergency has passed, understanding what worked and what didn't is crucial for future preparedness. AI systems can sift through mounds of post-event data to evaluate response effectiveness, identify bottlenecks, and suggest improvements. Machine learning can reveal insights into evacuation efficiency, resource distribution timeliness, and even the socio-economic impacts of the disaster. This analysis helps emergency management teams refine their protocols, ensuring that responses are consistently evolving and improving over time. While AI's immediate role might cease after the disaster ends, its influence persists, guiding better strategies and policies for subsequent events.

Artificial Intelligence in Agriculture

In today's rapidly evolving world of technology, AI is making waves across various sectors, bringing about significant transformations. One area where AI's impact is particularly profound is agriculture. By redefining traditional agricultural practices, AI is helping farmers enhance productivity and sustainability in ways that were unimaginable a few decades ago.

Let's start by looking at precision farming, which leverages AI to maximize resource efficiency and crop yields. This method involves using AI-driven tools to analyze data gathered from satellite imagery, sensors, and weather patterns, allowing farmers to make informed decisions about when and how much water, fertilizer, or pesticides to use. For instance, sensors can detect soil moisture levels across fields, guiding irrigation systems to distribute water only where it's needed, therefore conserving a precious resource. This targeted approach not only boosts productivity but also minimizes waste, contributing to sustainable farming practices.

A guideline for implementing these techniques involves choosing the right AI tools based on specific crops and environmental conditions. Farmers should begin by identifying key areas where data collection will most benefit their operations and ensure their staff is trained to interpret this information effectively. Regular evaluation of outcomes is essential to adjust strategies as needed.

Next up is automated farming equipment, which has revolutionized how tasks are performed on farms, slashing labor costs and reducing human error. Autonomous tractors and harvesters equipped with AI can operate day and night with minimal supervision, maintaining precision in planting, watering, and harvesting crops. This machinery can navigate vast fields using GPS and sensor technologies, ensuring that every inch of land is cultivated optimally. As a result, farm operations become more efficient, and workers can focus on more complex tasks that require human oversight.

Guidelines for adopting automated equipment include assessing the scale of your farming operations and determining specific tasks suitable for automation. It's crucial to invest in reliable technologies and regularly update software to keep machines functioning optimally. Additionally, engaging employees in training programs to manage these tools effectively ensures a smooth transition to high-tech methods.

AI also plays a critical role in pest and disease management. By analyzing historical data and current field conditions, AI systems can predict potential pest infestations before they occur, giving farmers the chance to take early preventive measures. Such predictive insights allow for timely interventions, whether it's deploying natural predators or applying appropriate pesticides, ultimately reducing crop losses. For instance, AI algorithms can identify patterns indicating an upcoming aphid outbreak, enabling the farmer to act swiftly and safeguard their crops.

To implement AI in pest management, start by integrating AI tools that match your specific needs and growing conditions. A combination of historical data and real-time monitoring provides a comprehensive picture, helping anticipate issues before they escalate. Ongoing updates of data inputs improve the system's accuracy and effectiveness over time.

Lastly, let's explore how AI contributes to supply chain optimization, decreasing food waste and improving market access. The agricultural supply chain is incredibly complex, involving multiple stages from production to distribution. AI can streamline these processes by predicting demand trends, optimizing logistics, and identifying bottlenecks. For example, AI can forecast which produce is likely to be in high demand during certain seasons, helping farmers plan their supply accordingly and reduce overproduction.

Moreover, AI-driven platforms facilitate better coordination between farmers, distributors, and retailers, ensuring that fresh produce reaches consumers efficiently. Through advanced analytics, stakeholders gain insights into market dynamics, which allows for strategic adjustments in pricing and inventory management, thus enhancing profitability and reducing food spoilage.

Farmers looking to optimize their supply chains with AI should start by evaluating their current distribution networks and identifying areas for potential improvement. Collaboration with technology providers who offer tailored solutions for agricultural supply chains can lead to greater efficiency gains. Establishing clear communication channels among all parties involved helps harness AI's full potential.

Protective Measures Using AI in Conservation Efforts

AI is transforming the way we protect wildlife and conserve the environment, offering innovative solutions that were unimaginable just a few decades ago. One such revolutionary application is poaching detection systems. These technologies are crucial in safeguarding endangered species from illegal hunting. By deploying AI-driven cameras and sensors in vulnerable areas, we can obtain real-time data that alerts conservationists to potential threats. This proactive approach not only prevents poaching by enabling rapid response teams to intervene but also collects valuable information on animal movements and behaviors. Such data helps conservation experts devise more effective strategies for protecting these majestic creatures.

In addition to deterring poachers, AI plays a significant role in monitoring habitats. It's vital to have an accurate picture of the ecosystem's health, as it directly impacts biodiversity and overall environmental balance. AI-powered drones and satellite imagery offer an unprecedented view of vast landscapes, analyzing changes over time. By processing this data, scientists can assess the effects of climate change, deforestation, and other human activities. Such insights guide targeted restoration efforts aimed at rehabilitating damaged ecosystems. For instance, if a particular region shows signs of deterioration, focused reforestation or anti-pollution measures can be implemented promptly, ensuring that natural habitats remain viable for future generations.

When considering broader environmental challenges, AI-powered climate models are proving invaluable. Policymakers rely on these advanced computational tools to craft strategies that mitigate climate impacts effectively. AI analyzes vast datasets from various sources like weather patterns, ocean currents, and greenhouse gas emissions. The result is a set of predictions that help leaders understand potential future scenarios. With this knowledge, governments can make informed decisions about policy directions, such as investing in renewable energy sources or implementing stricter emission controls. Moreover, accurate climate modeling aids in preparing communities for extreme weather events, which are becoming increasingly frequent due to global warming. By anticipating these situations, resources can be allocated efficiently to minimize harm to both people and the environment.

Beyond technical interventions, engaging local communities in conservation efforts is essential for sustainable success. AI-driven platforms are designed to educate and involve people in adopting greener practices. These platforms provide interactive content and real-time feedback on actions such as recycling, reducing energy consumption, or supporting biodiversity-friendly products. They encourage community participation by showcasing successful initiatives and providing practical tips. For example, a mobile app might track users' carbon footprints, suggesting personalized ways to reduce it. This not only raises awareness but also fosters a sense of responsibility and empowerment among individuals. When communities understand the impact of their actions, they are more likely to support conservation policies and initiatives, creating a ripple effect that benefits the planet.

The power of AI in wildlife protection and environmental conservation is multifaceted. By preventing poaching, monitoring habitats, informing policymakers, and engaging communities, AI equips us with the tools needed to tackle pressing ecological issues head-on. As AI technology continues to evolve, its applications will undoubtedly expand, opening up new possibilities for preserving our natural world and ensuring a sustainable future for all living beings. However, as we embrace these innovations, it is critical to address ethical concerns and ensure that AI deployment aligns with the best interests of both humans and the environment.

Summary and Reflections

Throughout this chapter, we've explored how AI is stepping up in various sectors, particularly in healthcare, by bringing innovative solutions to the table. From predictive analytics enabling early detection of health risks, to AI chatbots freeing up medical professionals for critical patient care, the impact on healthcare provision is hard to ignore. We've seen how AI-driven drug discovery speeds up the development of lifesaving medicines and how telehealth powered by AI ensures personalized and continuous care. In all these examples, AI isn't just a tool; it's reshaping our approach to medicine, making it more efficient and tailored to individual needs.

As we wrap things up, it's clear that while AI holds incredible promise, its deployment must be thoughtful, with proper guidelines and ethical standards. The challenge lies not only in adopting these technologies but also in balancing innovation with privacy and ethics. This transformation demands an open attitude towards change and a willingness to engage with new possibilities that AI offers. By keeping the conversation going and addressing concerns openly, we can harness AI's full potential to tackle complex global challenges, setting a new benchmark for future applications across different fields.

Chapter 14

Overcoming Skepticism Towards AI

O vercoming skepticism towards AI starts by addressing the common concerns and misunderstandings people have about this technology. Many folks see artificial intelligence as a mysterious entity, often fueling their apprehension with ideas of machines replacing humans in jobs or making decisions without human oversight. However, at its core, AI is simply a tool—a very powerful one—that, when used correctly, can enhance our capabilities and improve various aspects of life. It's all about learning to trust these systems and seeing them for what they really are: partners that can help us tackle some pretty big challenges.

In this chapter, we'll reassure those who feel cautious about adopting AI. We'll highlight real-world examples where AI has been successfully integrated into different fields, showing how it benefits industries like healthcare, education, logistics, and customer service. We'll also delve into public opinion shifts over time, exploring how initial fears have evolved into a more balanced acceptance as people see AI as a helpful companion rather than a threat. Furthermore, we'll discuss the importance of transparency in AI operations, ensuring that users understand how these technologies work, thus building trust and confidence. By the end of this chapter, readers will find a positive narrative around AI's role in society, moving beyond skepticism to appreciate the potential it holds for enhancing our daily lives.

Examples of Successful AI Integration

In today's rapidly advancing world, artificial intelligence (AI) is steadily demonstrating its value across a variety of sectors. Let's delve into some specific examples to understand how AI is truly benefiting different fields.

Firstly, consider healthcare, where AI is transforming diagnostics and treatment plans. Picture this: A patient comes in for routine testing, and the results are fed through an AI system trained on thousands of similar cases. The AI identifies anomalies much quicker and with higher accuracy than traditional methods, leading to faster diagnosis and targeted treatments. This precision means that diseases like cancer can be caught earlier, increasing the chances of successful outcomes. Hospitals worldwide are adopting AI tools that support doctors in decision-making processes, ultimately improving patient care and saving lives.

Now, let's shift our focus from the hospital to the classroom. Education systems worldwide are embracing AI to create personalized learning experiences. Imagine a classroom where every student receives a tailored learning plan, adapted in real-time to their strengths and weaknesses. AI technology can analyze a student's performance and adjust the material to keep them engaged, addressing challenges they might face along the way. This customization not only boosts engagement but enhances academic performance, as students receive the support they need precisely when they need it. Schools implementing these innovative solutions report higher levels of satisfaction among both students and teachers, creating a more effective learning environment.

Next, let's explore how AI is making waves in logistics. Logistics companies manage vast networks of vehicles and routes daily. With AI, these operations are becoming significantly more efficient. Advanced algorithms can process traffic data, weather conditions, and vehicle capacities to determine the optimal routes for delivery fleets. As a result, these companies see reductions in fuel consumption and overall operating costs. Trucks spend less time idling in traffic, deliveries are completed quicker, and customer expectations for speed and reliability are consistently met. Businesses utilizing AI-driven logistics find themselves staying ahead of competitors by slashing expenses and improving service quality.

Customer service is another area experiencing profound changes due to AI. Traditionally, customer service interactions were time-consuming, often ending with dissatisfied customers if issues weren't resolved promptly. Enter AI-driven customer support systems—chatbots and virtual assistants now handle routine inquiries, freeing up human representatives to tackle complex problems. These systems operate 24/7, providing users with instant responses, which translates to higher satisfaction rates. Companies employing AI in customer service not only enjoy happier customers but also better manage workloads and resources, allowing teams to focus on tasks that genuinely require human judgment and empathy.

Surveying Public Opinion Shifts on AI

In exploring public attitudes towards AI, we can see a fascinating journey marked by fear, acceptance, and even appreciation. Initially, much of the skepticism surrounding AI was driven by concerns over job displacement. Picture this: A world where machines replace human jobs, leaving many worried about their livelihoods. This anxiety was palpable in various sectors, from manufacturing to clerical work. The idea that robots and algorithms could outperform humans in tasks traditionally performed by us seemed daunting. However, as time has passed, this fear has gradually diminished.

The shift away from fear isn't just because AI hasn't replaced millions of workers overnight; it also relates to how we've adapted. Many organizations have found ways to use AI alongside humans rather than as a substitute. For instance, AI technologies are now often seen as tools that can automate repetitive tasks, allowing people to focus on more complex and creative aspects of their jobs. This evolution has helped soothe initial anxieties and shown AI as a partner rather than a competitor.

Recent surveys provide valuable insights into this changing mindset. An increasing number of people report feeling comfortable with AI technologies, indicating a growing reliance on and integration of these systems into everyday life. Think of voice assistants like Siri or Alexa, which have become household staples for managing schedules, controlling home environments, and seeking quick information. Survey data reveals that familiarity breeds comfort, with individuals who regularly interact with AI expressing higher trust levels.

Moreover, the demographic analysis suggests intriguing patterns regarding acceptance levels across different age groups. Younger generations, having grown up in a tech-savvy era, display greater openness toward AI advancements. These digital natives are accustomed to technology's rapid progression and view AI as a natural extension of innovation. In contrast, older generations may approach AI with more caution due to less exposure during formative years. Nevertheless, as technology becomes increasingly pervasive, even those initially hesitant are beginning to embrace its potential benefits.

Adding another layer to this narrative is the influence of high-profile success stories involving AI. When AI triumphs make headlines—be it defeating human champions in complex games, diagnosing diseases more accurately than doctors, or optimizing city infrastructure—the public perception shifts positively. These stories showcase AI's capabilities beyond theoretical speculation, providing tangible evidence of what it can achieve. As a result, trust in AI grows, bolstered by visible contributions to various fields.

Consider, for example, AlphaGo's victory over the world's best Go players. This event didn't just demonstrate AI's capabilities in understanding and strategizing within a complex game; it highlighted the potential for AI to tackle challenges previously thought exclusive to human intellect. Such victories spark curiosity and admiration, painting AI not just as a tool but as an ally capable of extraordinary feats.

It's also worth noting how AI plays roles in enhancing daily conveniences that many take for granted. From personalized recommendations on streaming services to fraud detection in banking, AI seamlessly operates behind the scenes, significantly improving user experiences. Many users unknowingly benefit from these applications, further integrating AI into the fabric of everyday life.

These combined factors create a nuanced picture of public attitudes towards AI. While initial skepticism fueled by job security concerns was understandable, evolving perceptions reflect a broader acceptance and willingness to engage with AI. It's a testament to human adaptability and the ability to embrace change when presented with clear benefits and effective integration strategies.

Transparency in AI Applications

In today's rapidly evolving technological landscape, skepticism toward AI often stems from a sense of uncertainty and lack of understanding. For many people, the idea that machines can learn and perform complex tasks feels abstract and, at times, intimidating. One powerful way to overcome this skepticism is through clarity and transparency in AI processes and operations. This approach not only demystifies AI but also fosters trust among diverse audiences who might be wary of embracing these technologies.

Take, for example, companies that effectively communicate their AI methodologies. When businesses are transparent about how their AI systems work, they create a sense of openness that builds public trust. People are more likely to embrace AI when they understand its capabilities and limitations. By openly discussing algorithms, data sources, and intended uses, companies can create an environment where consumers feel informed and secure. This direct communication helps dismantle the veil of mystery surrounding AI, presenting it as a tool designed for human benefit rather than an enigmatic force.

Furthermore, transparent AI practices have been repeatedly linked to increased consumer confidence. When users are privy to the inner workings of AI systems, they tend to feel more empowered and in control. This is particularly important as AI becomes integrated into everyday applications like online shopping, customer service, and even healthcare. By providing clear insights into how decisions are made, companies reassure consumers that AI serves their interests and respects their privacy. Real-world examples abound, such as financial institutions using AI to detect fraudulent activities. When these entities share their detection methods with customers, it fosters a safer, more trusting relationship.

Regulatory frameworks play a crucial role in promoting accountability through transparency in AI usage. By establishing guidelines that require organizations to disclose information about their AI processes, regulatory bodies ensure that businesses remain accountable for their actions. For instance, laws mandating data protection and algorithmic transparency can mitigate harmful biases in AI systems. This not only holds companies responsible but also protects consumers from potential ethical pitfalls. The discussion around these frameworks is significant in reinforcing public assurance that AI technologies will be developed and deployed responsibly.

As we navigate the complexities of AI adoption, it's evident that engaging the community in open discussions about AI strengthens stakeholder relationships. Creating forums for dialogue allows companies to address concerns, gather feedback, and adjust their strategies accordingly. This interaction is vital because it transforms skeptical audiences into active participants in AI development. By inviting questions and facilitating honest conversations, businesses demonstrate their commitment to addressing societal needs and preferences.

A practical guideline here would be to initiate initiatives that welcome public input and engagement. Companies should consider hosting workshops and seminars that offer interactive learning opportunities. Furthermore, by utilizing social media and online platforms, businesses can reach a broader audience, allowing for continuous dialogue and updates on AI advancements. Engaging stakeholders in this manner ensures that their voices are heard and valued, paving the way for more meaningful collaborations.

Another key element to fostering trust involves tangible demonstrations of AI's capabilities. When individuals witness firsthand how AI can improve efficiency, accuracy, or convenience, skepticism begins to wane. Consider AI-driven voice assistants or automated customer service chatbots, which ease daily routines and enhance user experience. These examples illustrate the practical benefits of AI, showcasing how transparency in operation leads to greater acceptance and trust.

Moreover, case studies highlight scenarios where transparency has led to positive outcomes. For instance, tech companies implementing AI for smart home devices often provide detailed documentation and regular updates on software changes. Such transparency assures users that their data is handled securely and used only for stated purposes. As a result, consumer confidence grows, transforming initial skepticism into appreciation for AI's utility.

Community involvement is another crucial aspect deserving attention. By creating spaces where individuals can express their opinions and concerns, the conversation around AI broadens significantly. Public consultations, Q&A sessions, and feedback surveys contribute to a comprehensive understanding of public sentiment. Through these avenues, companies gain insights into diverse perspectives, enabling them to tailor their AI solutions to better align with societal values.

To facilitate this process, it's helpful to establish channels for continuous engagement. Organizations should regularly update stakeholders on their AI projects and encourage constructive critiques. Additionally, collaboration with educational institutions can promote awareness and knowledge-sharing about AI's impact on various sectors. These efforts cultivate an informed community, ready to participate actively in shaping AI's future trajectory.

AI as a Partner Rather Than a Competitor

Artificial intelligence (AI) often conjures images of a dystopian future where robots replace humans in every job imaginable. However, this perception isn't entirely accurate. Instead, AI should be seen as a powerful ally that enhances our natural abilities and fosters collaboration across various fields. It's not about AI taking over; it's about how we can harness its potential to work alongside us, making our lives and work more efficient and exciting.

Consider the realm of healthcare, where AI-driven technologies are transforming patient care. In many hospitals, AI-powered systems assist doctors by analyzing medical data with incredible speed and accuracy. These systems don't replace doctors but instead serve as invaluable tools, enabling them to diagnose conditions faster and propose treatment plans with greater precision. By doing so, AI helps human professionals perform their jobs more effectively, fostering an environment where technology and human expertise coexist harmoniously.

Moreover, AI doesn't just process data—it's a master at quickening the pace of problem-solving, complementing human intuition with its impressive computational prowess. Think of scenarios in finance, where human analysts can leverage AI to sift through vast amounts of financial data swiftly, identifying trends and patterns that might otherwise go unnoticed. Here, AI acts as a reliable assistant, augmenting intuitive insights with hard data to make well-informed investment decisions. The symbiotic relationship between human intuition and AI's analytical capabilities showcases how these technologies can elevate productivity without replacing human roles.

Creative fields, too, are witnessing a transformation, thanks to AI's integration. Take, for instance, the advertising industry, where AI algorithms analyze consumer preferences to deliver personalized content. Successful organizations have recognized the potential of AI to amplify creative storytelling. While AI provides insights and suggestions based on data, human creativity remains at the forefront, crafting narratives that resonate emotionally with audiences. This blend of AI-driven analysis and human imagination leads to more compelling campaigns, illustrating the synergy between technology and creativity.

In industries like manufacturing, AI is increasingly being adopted to enhance productivity without eliminating jobs. Automated systems can manage repetitive tasks with precision, allowing human workers to focus on more complex, cognitively demanding activities. For example, in automotive factories, robots powered by AI handle assembly line jobs, ensuring accuracy and speed. Meanwhile, human workers engage in quality checks, innovation, and other vital tasks that require a nuanced understanding. This approach not only boosts production but also elevates the role of human workers to functions that challenge their intellect and creativity.

Encouraging broader acceptance of AI involves demonstrating successful partnership models across varied sectors. One such model is found in agriculture, where AI technologies analyze weather patterns and soil conditions to advise farmers. Precision farming, supported by AI, allows agricultural workers to optimize resources, reduce waste, and increase yields—showcasing how technology can revolutionize traditional practices. Rather than replacing the farmer, AI empowers them to make smarter decisions, turning age-old techniques into more sustainable and efficient processes.

To further shift perceptions, presenting real-world examples of AI partnerships strengthens the narrative of AI as a collaborative tool rather than a competitive threat. By highlighting companies and sectors that have embraced AI to complement human skills, skeptics can see tangible benefits. When organizations clearly illustrate how they employ AI to enhance—not overshadow—human capabilities, it encourages others to follow suit, gradually changing attitudes towards AI adoption.

In each scenario, the message is clear: AI is not here to take away jobs or diminish human value. On the contrary, when integrated thoughtfully, it can lead to more fulfilling work environments by freeing humans from mundane tasks and allowing them to engage in more meaningful endeavors. Imagine the possibilities when AI handles the grunt work, leaving us with time and energy to solve the bigger, more challenging puzzles.

As industries continue to explore how AI can augment human capabilities, it's essential to maintain an open dialogue. Discussing these models and success stories openly will help dispel fears and promote a more informed understanding of AI's positive impact. Bridging the gap between skepticism and acceptance requires evidence-based examples that demonstrate AI's role as a valuable partner in our collective future.

Continual Dialogue Addressing AI Fears

In today's rapidly evolving technological landscape, conversations about artificial intelligence (AI) are more important than ever. Yet, many people remain skeptical about AI's role and impact on society. To bridge this gap, we need to create a framework for ongoing discussions that both address concerns and promote understanding.

One effective way to stimulate these conversations is through open forums. These forums serve as vital platforms where individuals from all walks of life—be they professionals, enthusiasts, or skeptics—can engage in dialogue about AI's societal impacts. Such gatherings allow for transparent discussions, enabling people to voice their fears, anxieties, and hopes regarding AI. Attendees can ask questions, share personal experiences, and gain insights from experts in the field. By providing a space for direct interaction, open forums demystify AI. They help transform abstract concepts into relatable topics, offering reassurance to those wary of AI adoption.

To enhance public understanding further, educational campaigns play a crucial role. Many people perceive AI as a complex and intimidating subject steeped in technical jargon. Educational initiatives aim to simplify these intricate topics, making them accessible to a broader audience. Through workshops, online courses, webinars, and educational content, organizations can break down AI concepts into digestible pieces. This approach not only fosters comprehension but also piques curiosity, encouraging lifelong learning. With a clearer understanding of how AI works and its potential benefits, people's apprehension can shift towards informed interest and openness.

However, facilitating understanding is not a one-time activity. It's an ongoing process that requires constant engagement between communities and AI developers. Here, feedback loops become essential. By establishing channels for continuous dialogue, developers can gather valuable input from users and communities impacted by AI technologies. This feedback can be used to refine AI systems, ensuring that they align with community needs and ethical considerations. Additionally, feedback loops build trust, as they demonstrate a commitment to collaborative development and transparency. When people see their voices influencing AI evolution, it empowers them and strengthens the relationship between technology and society.

Another critical component of creating a comprehensive framework for AI discussions is addressing misinformation. In the age of information overload, misinformation about AI can spread quickly, fueling unnecessary fear and skepticism. Counteracting these myths is vital for shaping an informed public view. Organizations can launch fact-checking initiatives and collaborate with media outlets to ensure accurate reporting on AI-related stories. Moreover, community leaders and educators should be equipped to debunk common misconceptions about AI, highlighting its real capabilities and limitations. By proactively tackling misinformation, we can foster a culture of truth and clarity, transforming skepticism into well-informed scrutiny.

Each of these ideas highlights the importance of open, continued dialogue around AI. Open forums enable real-world connections between people and technology. Educational campaigns make the complex simple and understandable. Feedback loops create a partnership between developers and users, leading to better AI systems. Addressing misinformation ensures that public opinion is based on facts rather than fear. These elements combined form a solid foundation for ongoing conversations about AI.

Final Thoughts

As we wrap up this chapter, it's clear that AI is gradually becoming a valuable ally in different areas of our lives. From healthcare to education and logistics to customer service, AI is enhancing the way things get done. It's not just about machines taking over jobs; instead, AI works alongside us, helping us make smarter decisions and improving efficiency. Public attitudes are shifting too, as people become more familiar with AI's capabilities and see its positive impact firsthand. This evolving perspective opens up opportunities for dialogue, fostering a better understanding of how AI can complement human efforts rather than compete against them.

Moving forward, it's important to keep talking about AI openly. Transparency is key in building trust—when companies explain their AI processes and invite public input, it creates a sense of security and understanding. This openness encourages everyone, from tech enthusiasts to those new to AI, to engage with these technologies confidently. By showcasing real-world success stories and involving communities in the conversation, we can bridge the gap between skepticism and acceptance. The journey of integrating AI into society is ongoing, and by embracing open communication, we ensure that AI continues to serve as a helpful partner in our ever-changing world.

Chapter 15

Integrating AI with Human Values

Integrating AI with human values is a task that challenges us to consider technology's role in society from a fresh perspective. Instead of seeing AI as an isolated tool, it's essential to view it in light of the ethical and cultural frameworks that guide our everyday lives. This not only helps ensure AI aligns with societal norms but also encourages more responsible and mindful innovation. Imagine AI systems designed with an awareness of ethical principles or cultural sensitivities; they could transform sectors like healthcare, education, and urban development in ways that genuinely improve people's lives. By embedding ethical considerations into AI technologies, we can better prepare for the complex moral questions that arise as these systems become more ingrained in our daily activities.

In this chapter, you'll explore how insights from various branches of the humanities play a pivotal role in integrating AI with core human values. The fascinating influence of philosophy sets the stage by offering ethical guidelines and moral frameworks that help navigate AI's complexities. Through diverse philosophical lenses like utilitarianism and deontological ethics, developers are equipped to make informed decisions that align AI with societal values. We'll also delve into the importance of cultural narratives in shaping AI, ensuring that these technologies are inclusive and resonate with different communities worldwide. Interdisciplinary collaborations stand out as a key element in harmonizing technological advancement with humanity, bringing unique perspectives to the design process. Finally, learn about the indispensable role of moral reasoning frameworks in steering AI towards ethical behavior. With these ideas in mind, you'll gain a clearer understanding of how technology and human values can co-evolve, creating a future where AI enhances our shared human experience, rather than detracting from it.

The Role of Humanities in Shaping AI

In the journey of integrating artificial intelligence with human values, insights from the humanities play a crucial role. One compelling way humanities inform AI development is through philosophical frameworks. These frameworks offer ethical guidelines by providing different perspectives on our moral responsibilities toward technology and its users. By examining questions such as "What makes an action good or bad?" or "How do we prioritize conflicting interests?", philosophy helps us tackle the complexities of AI. For instance, utilitarianism might focus on the greatest good for the greatest number, while deontological ethics emphasizes duty and rules. These lenses give developers foundational principles to ensure AI technologies act in ways that align with societal values.

Philosophy also encourages a critical lens on AI decisions and their far-reaching implications. This approach allows us to question not only the methods but also the very purposes driving AI innovations. By fostering critical thinking, it helps anticipate challenges and ethical dilemmas that may arise from AI deployment. Imagine AI systems used in law enforcement; philosophical scrutiny can guide the creation of transparent, accountable algorithms that respect privacy and justice.

Cultural narratives are another vital dimension that the humanities bring into AI development. They influence how AI is perceived and accepted by embedding diverse societal values into its design. By telling stories that resonate with specific cultures, AI becomes more relatable and meaningful. Consider chatbots designed to assist in mental health care. If these AI tools are shaped by cultural insights, they could better understand and sympathize with users' experiences, offering support in culturally sensitive ways.

Including diverse cultural narratives in AI design also ensures inclusivity. This approach creates technologies that speak to varied identities, preferences, and traditions, rather than promoting a one-size-fits-all solution. A guideline worth noting is encouraging a range of voices in the brainstorming phase of AI projects. This means involving representatives from various communities early on, ensuring their values and needs are woven into AI systems from the start.

Furthermore, interdisciplinary collaborations between technologists and humanities scholars create richer, value-aligned AI solutions. When AI developers work alongside philosophers, sociologists, or anthropologists, they gain insights into human behavior, ethics, and culture. These collaborations spark innovative ideas that reflect broader societal values, making AI tools more attuned to the people who use them.

One example of successful interdisciplinary collaboration is in urban planning applications powered by AI. Partnering engineers with social scientists can lead to solutions that balance technical efficiency with community needs, enhancing livability and sustainability. Such teamwork underscores the importance of drawing on multiple fields to solve complex problems, highlighting how diverse expertise contributes to AI that respects and enhances human life.

Moral reasoning frameworks are indispensable when deploying AI. They help ensure that AI behaves ethically and reduces potential risks. Just like humans, AI systems must navigate complex moral landscapes. Moral reasoning offers a structured way to handle these challenges, allowing machines to make choices that adhere to ethical standards. For example, self-driving cars must weigh potential outcomes in split-second decisions. By incorporating moral reasoning frameworks, developers can program these vehicles to prioritize safety over speed, balancing various factors to minimize harm.

It's essential to recognize that moral reasoning isn't just about avoiding negative outcomes but about actively promoting positive ones too. Encouraging diverse narratives in the development process fosters inclusivity and strengthens moral reasoning. Creating an inclusive platform for dialogue among stakeholders—users, developers, ethicists —helps build AI that genuinely considers a variety of perspectives and ethical viewpoints.

For those skeptical about AI's role in society, understanding its potential benefits and pitfalls is key to fostering open dialogue. By illustrating how humanities-inspired approaches guide ethical AI development, we invite skeptics to appreciate the thoughtful integration of technology with human values. Such discussions help address hesitations and foster informed conversations about AI's place in modern life.

Balancing Technological Advancement with Humanity

In a world where AI technology is advancing at breakneck speed, it's crucial that we don't lose sight of the human values and dignity that should guide its implementation. Rapid technological development often has the potential to overshadow ethical considerations. When the focus is solely on innovation, it can be easy to overlook the implications these advancements have on society. This brings us to a vital point: the need for deliberate pacing in developing AI technologies. By intentionally slowing down and incorporating human-centered designs, we allow ourselves the time to consider, evaluate, and adapt the ethical frameworks that are necessary to protect our shared humanity.

Consider how AI is already integrated into everyday life, from smart assistants to complex algorithms driving decisions in sectors like healthcare and finance. These technologies affect real lives and must therefore be designed with a deep understanding of their social implications. If we fail to acknowledge the broader impact on societal norms and structures, we risk creating systems that exacerbate inequalities or unintentionally cause harm.

One key consideration is equitable access to AI technology. As developers and policymakers, it's essential to think about who benefits from these innovations and who might be left behind. Addressing questions like "Who has access to AI?" or "How will AI change job opportunities?" helps ensure that these technologies uplift rather than divide communities. For example, AI solutions deployed in healthcare should aim to improve access to medical services universally, not just for those in privileged positions.

Human oversight plays a critical role in ensuring that AI aligns with societal expectations and norms. Machines alone cannot navigate the complexities of human ethics and cultural differences. Thus, accountability becomes paramount. Ensuring there are individuals responsible for overseeing AI systems means that we are better equipped to intervene when things go awry. This oversight ties into the necessity for continuous training and development of human skills that are unique and irreplaceable by AI—skills like empathy, creative problem-solving, and moral discernment.

To sustain this balance between technology and human values, strategies must include active stakeholder engagement. Involving diverse voices from different backgrounds and fields fosters a more holistic approach to AI development. A variety of perspectives ensures that the technologies created are socially aware and inclusive. Regular evaluations of AI impacts are also essential. By continuously assessing the effects of AI systems in real-world contexts, stakeholders can make necessary adjustments to maintain alignment with societal values.

Guidelines for interdisciplinary collaborations highlight the importance of working across disciplines. Experts from fields such as sociology, psychology, law, and technology should work together to build ethical AI systems. When these disciplines collaborate, they bring various insights that enrich the technology's design process, contributing to AI that respects, preserves, and even enhances human dignity.

Creating moral reasoning frameworks within AI deployment provides a foundation for making ethical choices. These frameworks help developers embed ethical decision-making processes directly into AI systems. Implementing moral reasoning into AI algorithms can reduce ethical risks by ensuring that certain principles guide automated decisions. It's not about replacing human judgment but augmenting it, creating a symbiotic relationship where AI and humans work together harmoniously.

While case studies illustrating successful applications are useful for reinforcing these points, the overarching message remains—balancing technology with human values requires intentional effort. It's not enough to innovate for innovation's sake. Each advancement should be critiqued through the lens of what it adds to or takes away from human dignity.

Preserving Individuality in AI-Dominated Areas

In a world increasingly shaped by artificial intelligence (AI), the challenge of maintaining personal identity and individuality has never been more pressing. As AI systems become more embedded in our daily lives, there's a risk that personalization might overshadow individuality. Imagine opening your favorite app to see recommendations so finely tuned based on algorithms analyzing your previous choices, preferences, and behaviors, that you scarcely need to make any decisions yourself. While this level of personalization might seem convenient, it can blur the line between personalization and actual individuality, potentially subsuming our unique identities.

Personalization aims to customize experiences according to individual tastes, but it must be balanced against maintaining one's distinct identity. The difference lies in enhancing user experiences without overshadowing their identities. For instance, while streaming services suggesting movies based on past viewing habits is helpful, if it limits exposure to new genres or stories outside those preferences, it risks narrowing a person's worldview rather than broadening it. Thus, the goal should be to ensure that AI empowers users to retain their distinctiveness and explore new avenues rather than confining them to predetermined paths.

A significant challenge comes from algorithmic grouping, which can mistakenly prioritize conformity over individuality. Algorithms designed to efficiently categorize can sometimes result in stereotyping or homogenizing groups of people with similar traits or interests. This can lead to a loss of non-conforming perspectives when systems automatically favor what's popular or typical at the expense of diversity. Therefore, inclusivity and personalization should be paramount in AI design, offering diverse options instead of pushing users toward the most common choices. By prioritizing inclusivity, AI can better accommodate varied user identities, ensuring everyone remains authentic within digital interactions.

To counteract inherent biases in AI systems, it's crucial to utilize diverse data sets and implement robust feedback mechanisms. These biases often stem from historical data patterns and human prejudices inadvertently encoded into algorithms. For instance, an AI tasked with filtering job applications might unintentionally favor candidates from certain backgrounds if previous hiring data reflected those patterns. Addressing this requires incorporating a wide range of data points that reflect different demographics and experiences. Furthermore, feedback loops where users can report biases or inaccuracies help refine AI tools, making them more equitable and representative of varied identities.

Celebrating human creativity is another effective strategy to maintain individuality in an AI-dominated landscape. Humans possess an innate ability to innovate, express emotions, and create uniquely. While AI can automate tasks or generate content efficiently, it lacks the nuanced understanding and emotional depth that humans bring to creative processes. Supporting and emphasizing human creativity ensures unique ideas continue to flourish, resisting AI's potential for uniformity. Whether through art, writing, music, or innovative problem-solving, celebrating these human contributions highlights irreplaceable attributes that machines cannot replicate.

For example, consider the impact of AI in the art world. While AI can generate artworks, they lack the personal story, emotion, and intentionality that human artists infuse into their work. Human creativity is driven by personal experiences, cultural influences, and individual perceptions, resulting in pieces that resonate on a deeply personal level. Encouraging creativity not only preserves individuality but also reinforces the value of human expression in a tech-driven world.

Moreover, embracing one's uniqueness can inspire technological advancements that prioritize human-centered design. When individuals value their unique capabilities and perspectives, they become advocates for AI systems that support and enhance these qualities rather than diminish them. It encourages developers to build AI that understands and adapts to human needs, enhancing rather than overriding personal agency.

Taking a step back, it's clear that AI should complement, not replace, the elements that define us as individuals. Designing AI systems with these considerations involves creating spaces where technology serves as a tool to augment human capacities, not limit them. This way, we can enjoy the benefits of technological progress without losing the essence of who we are. By advocating for systems that honor individuality, society can leverage AI's potential while safeguarding the diverse tapestry of human identity.

Case Studies of Value-Driven AI Projects

When we talk about integrating AI with human values, it's essential to see how this plays out in real life. One great way to do that is by looking at AI projects designed for social good. These initiatives often tackle both humanitarian and environmental challenges, showcasing the incredible potential of technology when aligned with core humanistic values.

For instance, AI-driven tools are being used to improve healthcare delivery in underserved areas worldwide. By analyzing vast amounts of medical data, AI can help predict disease outbreaks or personalize treatment plans, ensuring that people receive care tailored to their specific needs. This not only saves time but also improves health outcomes, which is a powerful demonstration of technology enhancing our quality of life. Similarly, AI is making strides in environmental conservation. By analyzing satellite imagery, AI systems can monitor deforestation rates and help enforce measures against illegal logging, ultimately protecting our planet's precious resources.

At the heart of these efforts are ethical guidelines that form the backbone of trustworthy AI development. For an AI system to truly be in line with human values, transparency in decision-making is crucial. Imagine an AI application used in the justice system to determine bail. Without clear, understandable criteria for its decisions, public trust would erode quickly. That's why many organizations have adopted best practices ensuring that these technologies remain transparent and accountable. They open up their algorithms or publish reports detailing how decisions are made. Not only does this build trust, but it also encourages more institutions to adopt similar practices, setting a positive example across industries.

Furthermore, collaboration among diverse stakeholders has become increasingly common in AI projects that aim to promote societal well-being. Instead of working in isolation, tech companies often team up with non-profits, government agencies, and academic institutions to address complex societal issues. Take the example of AI in disaster response: various organizations come together to develop AI tools that predict natural disasters, enabling timely evacuations and resource distribution. This cross-sector partnership ensures that solutions are holistic, considering multiple perspectives and expertise, leading to stronger, more effective outcomes.

Another important aspect of integrating AI with human values is adopting user-centric development models. At first glance, it might sound like a buzzword, but its importance cannot be overstated. When users are involved in the ongoing development of a tool or service, they feel a sense of ownership and satisfaction. Their input helps refine the technology, ensuring it remains relevant and useful. By gathering feedback from end-users, developers can make improvements that better align with what people actually want and need. This iterative process benefits both users and creators, resulting in technology that adapts and evolves over time.

To bring all these elements together, imagine an AI project aimed at reducing food waste. Such an initiative could involve a collaborative effort between local governments, grocers, and tech companies to create an app powered by AI. The app could predict supply-demand trends, helping stores stock more efficiently while offering consumers tips on using leftovers creatively. Throughout the project, ethical guidelines would ensure that data privacy is respected, maintaining consumer confidence. And by engaging with users for continuous feedback, the app could fine-tune its features, providing even greater utility.

Synergizing Cultural Sensibilities with AI Innovation

In today's rapidly advancing technological landscape, integrating artificial intelligence with human values is not just a visionary ideal but a necessary path toward crafting innovative and socially responsible outcomes. At the heart of this integration lies the vital role of aligning AI solutions with cultural values, a process that is crucial for ensuring technology serves communities in ways that are both meaningful and relevant.

Imagine you're developing an AI application intended to assist farmers in a rural area. A one-size-fits-all solution might overlook local farming methods, traditional knowledge, or community practices. By designing AI systems with sensitivity to cultural contexts, developers can enhance acceptance and usability. This approach shows respect for local nuances, allowing AI technologies to be seen not as foreign intrusions but as harmonized tools that enrich the local way of life. For example, AI-driven apps designed for language translation can include local dialects, thus preserving linguistic heritage and making these tools more user-friendly.

Speaking of preservation, AI's role in documenting and celebrating cultural heritage cannot be overemphasized. Around the world, languages and traditions face extinction pressures due to globalization and modernization. AI projects aimed at cultural preservation are fought on the front lines to combat this loss. These projects digitize folklore, music, dances, and languages, offering new hope and visibility to endangered cultures. Consider how AI-generated digital archives allow future generations to access and appreciate their rich cultural tapestries that might otherwise fade into obscurity. The positive societal roles of such projects demonstrate the power of AI not only as a modernizing force but as a guardian of history and identity.

Moreover, the journey towards culturally aware AI extends into who builds it—a point vividly stressed by the diversity within development teams. When teams consist of individuals from various cultural backgrounds, they bring a wider range of perspectives and experiences to the table. This diversity is instrumental in countering mainstream biases, which often plague AI systems trained predominantly on homogenous data. For instance, facial recognition technology has historically shown bias against people with darker skin tones. Diverse teams are more likely to recognize such disparities and work proactively to address them, creating applications that are more sensitive and inclusive. By diversifying team composition, we open doors to creative problem-solving that reflects the richness of human experience.

The concept of collaborative cultural innovation labs takes this idea even further. These labs act as melting pots where technologists, cultural experts, artists, and community members converge to co-create AI solutions that genuinely reflect cultural values. Within these spaces, technology isn't developed in isolation but as part of a dialogue —a conversation between the past and the present, tradition and innovation. Imagine a lab that brings together indigenous craftspersons and AI developers to create an app that teaches traditional crafts through augmented reality. Such collaborations demonstrate the transformative potential when technology is interwoven with cultural essence, spurring solutions that are not only innovative but also respectful and celebratory of cultural diversity.

Guidelines for embracing collaboration in AI development emphasize openness and inclusivity. Cultural innovation labs should be designed to operate on the principles of mutual respect, active listening, and shared objectives. Stakeholders need transparent roles and responsibilities, fostering a culture of trust and shared ownership. Initiating these projects with clear, culturally sensitive goals ensures that all voices are heard and valued, avoiding the pitfalls of misunderstanding or undervaluation of certain cultural aspects. By engaging with diverse groups, these labs prompt sustainable innovation that doesn't just take from the community but gives back, strengthening the bond between technology and culture.

Final Thoughts

As we wrap up this chapter, it's clear how essential it is to ensure AI development aligns with our society's core values. We've delved into the ways humanities provide crucial insights, from offering ethical guidelines through philosophy to embedding cultural narratives into AI design. It's about making technology not just innovative but also relatable and culturally sensitive. By involving diverse voices early on, we can make sure that AI respects different identities and traditions, fostering solutions that truly cater to a broad spectrum of societal needs.

Moving forward, the importance of balancing technological advancement with humanity can't be overstated. As AI becomes more prevalent in our daily lives, accountability and inclusivity should be at the forefront. Developers and policymakers need to think deeply about who benefits from these innovations and how they impact us all. Human oversight remains vital in navigating the intricacies of implementing AI ethically and effectively. Collaborations across disciplines enrich AI systems, ensuring they enhance rather than diminish our inherent human dignity. Through continuous dialogue and evaluation, we can create AI that stands as a testament to our shared values and respect for individual uniqueness.

Chapter 16

AI in Entertainment and Gaming

E xploring how artificial intelligence (AI) is reshaping the entertainment and gaming industry promises a thrilling journey into uncharted digital territories. The magic of AI lies in its ability to transform ordinary game landscapes into vibrant, intelligent worlds that react and adapt to every player move. Picture yourself navigating a game where your actions not only determine the unfolding story but also influence the environment around you. This kind of dynamic interaction showcases the significant leap from traditional linear gameplay to something much richer and more immersive. With AI, games can now offer a personalized adventure that's unique to each user, making every gaming session a fresh experience.

In this chapter, we dive into the fascinating ways AI revolutionizes the creation and enjoyment of entertainment. Expect insights into how AI enhances augmented reality, providing more than just fun but truly interactive experiences. You'll see examples where AI-generated content breathes life into virtual environments and discover innovations like procedural content generation, which ensures that no two gameplays are ever the same. As we explore further, we'll uncover how AI doesn't stop at enhancing games; it stretches its potential to live events and streamlining interactions, offering a glimpse into a future where entertainment is as unpredictable and exciting as our imaginations allow. Join us as we break down the barriers between fantasy and reality, all thanks to the ingenious applications of AI technology.

Augmented Reality and AI Interactions

In today's rapidly evolving world of entertainment, augmented reality (AR) and artificial intelligence (AI) are two groundbreaking technologies that have come together to create more engaging experiences than ever before. The synergy between AR and AI is setting the stage for dynamic interactions that captivate audiences by immersing them in digital environments blended seamlessly with the real world. Understanding this synergy is crucial for grasping how these technologies can transform not just how we entertain ourselves, but also how we interact with digital content on a personal level.

To start, let's break down how AR and AI work together to deliver these immersive experiences. Augmented reality enhances our perception of the real world by overlaying digital information onto it. This could be anything from visual displays like 3D models and animations to auditory enhancements such as sound effects or music. Meanwhile, AI comes into play by enabling these interactions to be intelligent and adaptable. Through real-time data processing, AI analyzes user behaviors and environmental cues to modify AR elements accordingly, creating a personalized experience for each user. For instance, an AI could alter the storyline of an AR-based game based on how a player interacts with their surroundings or the choices they make, resulting in a truly unique adventure every time.

One successful example of the power of AI-enhanced AR is Pokémon GO, a mobile game that took the world by storm. Leveraging geolocation and image recognition, this game brought beloved Pokémon characters into the real world through players' smartphone screens. But what kept users engaged were the AI-driven updates that evolved the game over time. New features, events, and challenges motivated players to return to the game repeatedly, demonstrating the importance of continuous innovation powered by AI. The game's capacity to adapt to changes in user patterns and interests highlights how AI plays a pivotal role in maintaining user engagement over extended periods.

Beyond gaming, we're seeing the potential of AR and AI integration stretch into other areas of entertainment, particularly social interaction platforms. Looking forward, advancements in these technologies could lead to seamless integration of AR with social media, providing even richer interactive experiences. Imagine attending a virtual concert with friends from around the globe where you could not only watch the performance but interact with digital elements corresponding to the real-time actions at the venue. AI could predict attendees' preferences, suggesting tailored experiences or highlighting parts of the show that align best with individual tastes. This type of personalized content delivery would not only enhance user satisfaction but also drive deeper engagement across communities.

Moreover, AI is expected to contribute significantly to privacy and security within AR environments. As augmented reality starts playing a bigger role in our daily lives, safeguarding personal data becomes paramount. AI can monitor data exchanges ensuring that users' information remains secure while offering transparency about how their data is used within these experiences. By addressing these concerns, AI will promote safer adoption of AR technology by wider audiences who might otherwise be reluctant due to privacy issues.

While it's exciting to speculate on future trends, the current landscape already offers myriad ways in which AI propels AR into unprecedented territories. Whether it's in entertainment, education, or other sectors, the possibilities seem endless. For instance, educational applications utilizing AI-driven AR could revolutionize learning by making it possible for students to explore historical sites or conduct complex science experiments in a controlled virtual setting, fostering an environment where education is both informative and engaging.

Creating Realistic Game Worlds with AI

In the realm of gaming, AI has become a powerful ally in crafting immersive and realistic environments that captivate players. One way AI achieves this is through procedural content generation. Imagine playing a game where every landscape you explore is unique, offering fresh challenges and unseen vistas each time you play. This isn't fantasy; it's how procedural content generation works. AI algorithms can create sprawling worlds filled with diverse terrains, intricate structures, and ever-changing ecosystems. This not only boosts replayability but also keeps players engaged by providing novel experiences each time they return to the game.

A key advantage of procedural content generation is its ability to surprise players. Unlike static game levels, these dynamic environments evolve with each playthrough. For instance, while exploring a forest in a role-playing game, players might encounter different weather conditions or wildlife behaviors depending on their previous actions or choices. This adaptability makes players feel like they're part of a living, breathing world rather than just navigating a pre-set path.

Additionally, AI aids in making game environments adaptable to player actions—a feature known as environmental adaptability. This capability allows the game world to respond in real-time, adapting to decisions made by the players. Think of it as the game world's version of cause and effect. If a player sets off a chain reaction by destroying a dam, the landscape may flood, reshaping the terrain and adding new layers of challenge and exploration. These responsive elements make the game world more interactive, fostering deeper immersion and providing a personalized experience that resonates with players.

Furthermore, AI-driven graphics significantly enhance realism in gaming. Visuals are often the first thing that draws players into a game, and AI plays a crucial role in improving these graphics to such an extent that they border on photorealistic. By employing advanced machine learning techniques, developers can fine-tune textures, lighting, and character animations in a way that's both efficient and incredibly detailed. For example, AI can enhance facial expressions, making characters appear more lifelike and emotionally engaging. This level of detail invites players to lose themselves in the game's universe, fully investing their attention and emotions.

The impact of AI on graphics extends beyond mere visual appeal. As the graphics become more lifelike, players find themselves more emotionally connected to the game. Realistic settings and characters encourage players to suspend disbelief and invest their emotions into the story being told. This emotional engagement enriches the overall gaming experience and elevates storytelling within games to an art form.

Moreover, AI technology allows developers to push the boundaries of what's possible in game visuals without demanding excessive hardware resources from players. Through optimization processes driven by AI, games can maintain stunning graphics even on less powerful systems, ensuring a wider audience can enjoy these immersive experiences. This democratization of high-quality visuals broadens access to compelling interactive storytelling for gamers worldwide.

Guidelines for developers interested in harnessing procedural content generation include understanding the balance between randomness and structure. While endless variety is enticing, maintaining coherence in the narrative and geography of the game world ensures that procedurally generated content still aligns with the overall theme and storyline. Additionally, incorporating feedback loops may help refine the AI's decision-making process, gradually improving quality and responsiveness over multiple iterations.

AI-Facilitated Live Content Generation

Artificial Intelligence (AI) has become a game-changer in the realm of live entertainment and interactive content generation, transforming the way audiences experience events. One of the most remarkable impacts of AI is seen in its ability to enhance live events with real-time visual and audio effects. Imagine attending a concert where the lighting changes dynamically in synchronicity with the music or watching a sports event where the replays are instantly analyzed and enhanced with graphics that help you better understand the plays. These experiences are made possible through AI technologies that process large volumes of data rapidly to create seamless and captivating visuals and sounds. By doing so, they elevate the overall audience experience, making each event unforgettable.

AI doesn't stop at enhancing what happens on stage or screen; it turns the viewing process itself into an interactive adventure. Interactive streaming platforms use AI to tailor content based on viewer preferences, significantly increasing user engagement. For example, when you watch a streaming service, AI algorithms analyze your viewing habits—what types of shows you prefer, what time you usually watch, and even how much of the content you typically consume in one sitting. With this information, AI can suggest new shows, change the ads displayed during programs, or even adjust streaming quality to match your internet connection.

Moreover, the rise of AI-driven interactive streams means that audiences are no longer passive observers but active participants in their viewing experience. Consider live-streamed video games where AI can adapt the difficulty level in real-time based on how players are performing, keeping them challenged yet entertained. Or imagine being able to vote for certain actions in reality TV shows, influencing outcomes as they happen. This level of interaction not only keeps viewers engaged but also fosters a sense of inclusion and excitement, as audiences feel like they have a stake in the entertainment.

User-generated content is another area where AI is leaving a significant mark by facilitating and encouraging more audience participation. Traditionally, creating content required technical skills and resources that were out of reach for many people. However, AI tools now simplify this process, allowing individuals to create high-quality videos, music, or even virtual art without needing extensive expertise. For example, AI software can assist with editing videos, automatically trimming awkward pauses or suggesting the best filter to enhance imagery, which empowers users to produce polished content with minimal effort.

By democratizing content creation, AI not only enriches the pool of available entertainment but also encourages diverse perspectives and voices. In live shows, this means that fan art, videos, or remixes can be incorporated into the event itself, creating an inclusive atmosphere where fans directly influence the entertainment landscape. Such participation builds community and loyalty, as fans see their contributions valued and showcased.

For instance, some live concerts invite fans to submit their renditions of songs or dance routines ahead of time, which AI then curates into a montage played during the show. This approach not only celebrates individual creativity but also strengthens the bond between performers and their audiences. As a result, entertainment becomes a collaborative endeavor rather than a one-sided delivery.

Guidelines for harnessing these AI capabilities efficiently can help both creators and consumers maximize their experiences. To appreciate real-time AI content creation, it's essential to keep an open mind about how technology can complement creative aspects rather than overshadow them. Embracing AI doesn't mean replacing human talent with machines; instead, it's about augmenting artist efforts with tech-driven insights to reach greater artistic heights.

When engaging with interactive streams and gaming, viewers and players can benefit from understanding how AI customizes experiences. This awareness can lead to heightened anticipation and curiosity, as audiences explore personalized journeys crafted just for them. Knowing that AI adapts content based on their feedback and choices can inspire users to engage more deeply, trying various options to see different outcomes.

Finally, embracing user-generated content backed by AI requires fostering a supportive community. Removing barriers to creation allows everyone to participate and contribute meaningfully. Encouraging diverse input benefits all stakeholders, as new ideas emerge from unexpected places, enriching the entertainment tapestry.

Adaptive AI Opponents in Gaming

In the world of gaming, AI has become a pivotal player, no longer just a feature but an integral part of creating engaging and challenging experiences. At the forefront of these advancements is the concept of dynamic difficulty adjustment (DDA). Imagine playing a game where the challenge consistently matches your skill level; this is precisely what DDA achieves. By analyzing the player's performance in real-time, AI can adjust the difficulty settings to ensure that players are neither overwhelmed by impossible tasks nor bored by too-easy opponents.

This system uses algorithms that monitor various metrics such as success rates, completion times, and error frequencies. A guideline for implementing effective DDA would be to continuously gather data throughout gameplay, allowing the AI to make subtle changes without breaking the immersion or interrupting the flow of the game. For instance, if you find yourself breezing through levels, the AI might introduce more complex puzzles or tougher adversaries. Conversely, if you're struggling, it might provide additional hints or reduce enemy aggression. This adaptability keeps players engaged and makes games accessible to both novices and veterans. It strikes a balance, making each session feel fresh and rewarding, avoiding the common pitfall of stagnation.

Beyond adjusting difficulty, AI enriches gameplay by providing advanced strategical opponents. Gone are the days when enemies followed predictable patterns easily memorized by players. Today's AI-powered opponents can learn from players' tactics, developing sophisticated strategies and counter-tactics. These intelligent opponents force players to think on their feet and refine their own strategies. A practical example is seen in strategy games where AI doesn't just react but anticipates player moves, offering formidable competition. In competitive sports games, this could translate into virtual athletes that adapt their playstyles based on your team's weaknesses, making every match uniquely challenging.

A guideline here would be ensuring the AI not only analyzes immediate player actions but also adjusts over time. Implementing machine learning techniques allows the AI to evolve its strategies, creating a learning curve that scales with the player's progress. This capability turns gaming into an ongoing chess match between human ingenuity and digital intellect, adding layers of depth and satisfaction each time players overcome these virtual adversaries.

AI is not limited to opposition roles; it also thrives as a cooperative partner in gameplay. Consider scenarios where AI-controlled characters work alongside players, coordinating efforts to achieve shared objectives. Such roles have been effectively utilized in team-based games, where AI teammates adapt to player strategies, filling in gaps and enhancing overall effectiveness. This collaborative AI must be able to understand context, adjust to unexpected changes, and support human players seamlessly. Imagine playing as part of a squad, where the AI teammate learns your tactics over time, maybe picking up on your preferences for stealth or direct confrontation, and adjusting its style accordingly.

A guideline for developing cooperative AI includes ensuring consistent communication between AI and player inputs. This requires employing algorithms that can interpret player commands and contextual cues accurately. Regular updates based on player feedback can help fine-tune these interactions, maintaining the sense of strategic partnership.

The inclusion of adaptive AI in games isn't just about improving mechanics; it's about enriching the entire gaming experience. Players often find joy in overcoming obstacles, savoring the moments of triumph after pushing through difficult challenges tailored perfectly to their skills. Moreover, by offering diverse AI personalities—some with aggressive tactics, others more defensive or cunning—developers can create games with rich, immersive worlds where each playthrough feels unique. Advanced AI opponents and collaborators promote creativity and problem-solving among players, encouraging them to experiment with different approaches.

Finally, beyond entertainment, these AI systems set a precedent for other applications, demonstrating how intelligent technology can enhance user interaction in various fields. By tailoring responses, predicting behaviors, and offering personalized experiences, AI's role in gaming foreshadows its potential across multiple sectors, paving the way for future innovations.

Personalized Gaming Experiences Using AI

In the ever-evolving world of gaming, artificial intelligence (AI) plays a pivotal role in customizing experiences to fit individual user preferences. Gone are the days when games followed a one-size-fits-all format; today, AI is reshaping the landscape by tailoring narratives and challenges to suit each player's unique style and interests. This level of personalization is accomplished through careful analysis of user behavior, allowing AI systems to craft gaming experiences that feel both engaging and exclusive.

User behavior analysis forms the backbone of this personalized approach. By observing how players interact with different game elements—such as their choices in dialogue, strategies in combat, or paths taken in exploration—AI systems can gather insights into what excites and motivates them. Once AI understands a player's preferences, it can adjust the game trajectory accordingly. This could mean introducing more puzzles for strategy enthusiasts or creating high-stakes battles for those who thrive on action. In doing so, AI ensures that every session feels rewarding and aligned with the player's desires. For instance, if a player consistently chooses peaceful resolutions over conflict, the AI might present scenarios where diplomacy offers rich narrative rewards.

This tailored experience extends beyond immediate gameplay mechanics, delving into the realm of dynamic storytelling. Unlike traditional static storylines, these adaptable narratives evolve based on player decisions, enhancing emotional engagement. Imagine a game where each decision branches into new possibilities, crafting a story unique to the player's choices. This mechanism not only keeps players invested in the unfolding tale but also deepens the emotional connection to characters and outcomes. The unpredictability of such games encourages players to return, eager to explore alternative paths and endings.

Guidelines here serve to ensure balance and coherence in these dynamic storylines. By setting parameters around key plot points and character arcs, AI can maintain a compelling and logical flow, regardless of player decisions. This structured flexibility allows for creativity without sacrificing the integrity of the narrative. Moreover, it empowers developers to weave complex stories that still remain accessible, ensuring all players, regardless of their technical understanding, can fully enjoy the experience.

Community-driven personalization represents another exciting frontier in AI-enhanced gaming. More than just consumers, players become active contributors to game content. Through direct feedback, modding communities, and user-generated content, AI incorporates community preferences into the broader gaming ecosystem. This collaboration results in games that are continually evolving, shaped by the players themselves.

For instance, consider a scenario where players create custom quests or characters that can be integrated into the main storyline. With AI filtering and refining these contributions, the game becomes a living entity that reflects the collective imagination of its community. Such involvement fosters a sense of ownership and investment among players, enriching their connection to the game.

In practice, guidelines ensure that community-sourced content aligns with the overall game theme and quality standards. By automating the vetting process, AI helps maintain a consistent aesthetic and narrative tone across diverse user creations. This encourages innovation while safeguarding the game's core identity, allowing players to push creative boundaries without detracting from the game's original concept.

The transformative impact of AI in customizing gaming experiences speaks to its potential within the broader entertainment sector. Beyond providing mere entertainment, these personalized experiences promote a deeper level of interaction between the user and the technology. As AI continues to advance, it promises even greater innovations in how we engage with digital content, blurring the lines between creator and consumer in unprecedented ways.

Concluding Thoughts

As we've explored, AI is fundamentally reshaping the landscapes of gaming and interactive experiences. By merging with augmented reality, AI creates worlds that respond to each player's unique style, offering personalized adventures that were unimaginable a few years ago. From keeping us engaged with ever-changing environments in games like Pokémon GO to offering real-time adaptive challenges through dynamic difficulty adjustment, these technologies are pushing the boundaries of what's possible in entertainment. We've also seen how AI enhances live events and social interactions, making our experiences richer and more immersive. Whether it's crafting lifelike game graphics or enhancing privacy in AR spaces, AI is a key player in our digital future.

Looking ahead, it's clear that AI's influence will only grow, setting new standards for how we engage with digital content. For those curious about AI but wary of its implications, understanding how it enhances rather than replaces human creativity can offer some reassurance. As lifelong learners and skeptics alike, the more we embrace these innovations, the more we can steer them toward positive outcomes. While AI continues to evolve, the potential it holds for transforming not just gaming but various aspects of life remains vast and exciting. It's an ongoing journey of discovery, one where technology opens doors to endless possibilities while still valuing human input and creativity.

Chapter 17

Overcoming Challenges in AI Implementation

I mplementing AI in any organization can be a bit like taking on a challenging puzzle. Each piece represents a different obstacle—resources, scale, and adaptation—yet when combined correctly, they create a powerful picture of success. For small organizations, these challenges can seem daunting at first. Limited budgets, scaling issues, and the inherent resistance to change often feel like significant roadblocks on the path to harnessing AI's potential. However, just because the road is bumpy doesn't mean it's impassable. By understanding the nature of these challenges, small businesses can begin to unlock practical solutions tailored to their unique circumstances.

In this chapter, we'll dive into the practical hurdles that organizations face when trying to bring AI technologies into their everyday operations. From allocating resources wisely and tackling scalability concerns to managing change within the workforce, this exploration provides clear strategies for navigating these obstacles. Whether you're part of a team dipping its toes into the world of AI or leading an entire organization through the transition, this chapter offers game plans that are not only actionable but also adaptable to various organizational needs. Plus, we'll cover the benefits of phased investments and how leveraging open-source projects can offer flexibility and cost reduction. Ready to tackle these challenges head-on? Let's get started!

Technical Limitations Faced in Small Organizations

Navigating the dynamic landscape of AI technology presents unique challenges for small organizations. Resource allocation, scalability issues, and resistance to change all emerge as significant obstacles, yet each can be addressed with strategic planning and a clear understanding of organizational capabilities.

Firstly, resource allocation is a critical concern. Small organizations frequently operate within limited budgets, which can make investing in AI technologies seem daunting. With tight financial constraints, these businesses often have to prioritize their spending, and sometimes, AI may not top the list. However, ignoring AI can also mean missing out on its potential benefits. To navigate this issue, assessing the exact needs of the organization is essential. Businesses should start by evaluating which areas can benefit most from AI implementation. For instance, if customer service enhancement or streamlining operations is crucial, prioritizing AI investment in those areas can lead to noticeable improvements without straining resources.

Additionally, phased investments can be a pragmatic approach. Instead of fully committing large sums upfront, smaller organizations might consider incremental adoption, which allows them to manage costs effectively and observe early returns on investment before expanding further. By carefully selecting cost-effective tools and planning expenditures over time, organizations can align with long-term strategic goals while respecting budget limitations.

Scalability also presents a notable challenge for smaller entities. Many AI solutions are designed with larger enterprises in mind, providing extensive features that may not be suitable or necessary for smaller players. This mismatch can create an environment where small organizations feel left behind. The key to overcoming this is identifying and adopting scalable AI solutions that cater specifically to smaller businesses. Small organizations should research and choose adaptable tools that allow them to scale their AI capabilities as they grow. Opting for cloud-based AI services is one viable pathway, as these options often offer customizable packages that can evolve alongside the organization's needs.

Moreover, leveraging open-source AI projects can provide flexibility and reduce costs, enabling experimentation without significant financial commitments. Engaging with communities around these projects can uncover additional insights and best practices, further empowering smaller organizations to integrate AI more efficiently.

Adaptation to change is another significant hurdle that smaller organizations face. AI integration demands a cultural shift, and resistance can stem from employees who fear job displacement or lack understanding of how AI will impact their roles. Cultivating an organizational culture that embraces change involves transparent communication about the intended benefits and impacts of AI. Clear narratives help demystify AI technologies and alleviate concerns, encouraging staff to view AI as a tool for enhancement rather than replacement.

Training programs play an indispensable role in facilitating this transition. By equipping employees with the needed skills through workshops and continuous learning opportunities, smaller organizations can ensure that their workforce remains agile and capable of leveraging AI technologies. These initiatives help build confidence among employees, making them active participants in the AI journey rather than passive observers.

It's also beneficial to highlight small successes within the organization as AI begins to take effect. Sharing stories of how AI has improved processes or outcomes reinforces the value it brings and fosters a positive attitude towards further technological advancements. Managers and leaders must act as champions for AI adoption, guiding teams through changes and reinforcing the commitment to innovation. Open forums where team members can voice opinions and share experiences regarding AI integration encourage dialogue and collective problem-solving, forming a supportive environment for transformation.

Integrating Legacy Systems with AI Technology

Navigating the integration of AI technologies into existing systems can feel like a labyrinth of technical challenges. One prominent issue is compatibility with legacy systems, which are often not designed to communicate effectively with modern AI technologies. Legacy systems can be old software or outdated hardware that an organization relies on but cannot easily replace. This mismatch creates data interoperability issues, as these older systems might not handle the data formats and protocols used by newer AI solutions.

Imagine trying to fit a round peg into a square hole—that's what it's like when you try to get traditional systems to interact with cutting-edge AI applications without any assistance. The remedy? Middleware solutions. Middleware serves as a bridge, facilitating communication between disparate systems so they can work together seamlessly. It's kind of like a translator for tech that ensures both sides understand each other perfectly. However, implementing middleware isn't just a copy-paste solution; it involves careful planning, selecting tools that align well with both your existing infrastructure and the AI technologies you plan to deploy.

Another layer of complexity comes from the costs associated with AI adoption. Retrofitting, or modifying existing systems to accommodate new technologies, can be financially daunting. Organizations must evaluate whether the benefits of such an investment justify the expense. This is where Return on Investment (ROI) analysis becomes crucial. Before jumping in, it's essential to conduct a thorough cost-benefit analysis. Ask yourself, "What value will AI bring to our operations?" and "Is this value greater than the cost of implementation?"

Think about the potential impact on efficiency, productivity, or even customer satisfaction. For instance, incorporating AI-driven automation could significantly speed up processes that were once painstakingly slow. But remember, it's not just about immediate gains. Consider the long-term implications and opportunities for growth that AI could unlock for your business. While the initial financial outlay may seem steep, the benefits often pay off over time—if you've done your homework.

Data migration presents yet another hurdle. Transitioning to AI systems frequently involves moving large volumes of data from existing repositories to new frameworks. This process must be handled with utmost care to maintain data integrity. Imagine photocopying a 100-page document; now imagine if some words were smudged or entirely missing. That's what can happen to your data if proper migration practices aren't followed. Data loss or corruption can lead to costly mistakes and decision-making errors.

To tackle these challenges, organizations should establish strict data governance policies during migration. It's akin to having rules in place that everyone follows to make sure nothing important gets lost in the shuffle. This governance includes setting up protocols for data validation, verification, and maintaining consistency across different platforms.

Moreover, consider using advanced tools and strategies that ensure seamless data transfer. These tools can automate parts of the migration process, minimizing human error and safeguarding precision. Additionally, investing in training staff to manage these technologies efficiently is invaluable. Employees should be equipped with the knowledge to troubleshoot and respond rapidly to any issues that arise during and after integration.

Data Scarcity and Quality Issues

Data is the backbone of any AI project, and understanding its limitations can significantly impact the success of implementing AI technologies. For smaller businesses that don't have access to extensive datasets, the lack of relevant data can become a significant concern. These organizations often struggle with creating robust AI solutions due to limited information. The absence of large volumes of data hinders training AI systems, which rely heavily on diverse datasets to function effectively. In simple terms, without enough data, an AI system may not learn well enough to make accurate predictions or provide valuable insights.

This limitation poses a challenge, especially for startups or smaller enterprises looking to harness AI's potential. They might not have years of customer interaction data or vast amounts of sales transactions to draw from, unlike larger competitors. This disparity creates barriers in developing AI models that require substantial and varied input data to optimize performance. Smaller companies might find themselves at a disadvantage, unable to fully realize AI capabilities due to this gap. Hence, identifying strategies that address these shortfalls is crucial.

One practical approach to mitigating data scarcity is focusing on data quality. High-quality data can often compensate for lower quantities by providing more reliable inputs for AI systems. Ensuring data quality involves setting up rigorous protocols for collecting timely, relevant, and accurate data. Imagine trying to teach a machine to understand language. If you feed it sentences full of errors or outdated words, it will struggle to comprehend or generate useful responses. Similarly, for AI projects, precise data collection is non-negotiable.

Organizations should establish strict procedures for data validation and regularly update their databases to reflect current realities. This involves maintaining clear guidelines on what constitutes acceptable data, training employees involved in data entry or management on best practices, and using technology to automate error-checking processes. These steps help ensure that the data feeding into AI systems is as pristine as possible, allowing them to operate more effectively even when dataset size is not optimal.

Moving beyond just quality, another effective tactic is data enrichment. This process involves enhancing existing data to increase its value and utility. One way organizations can do this is through feedback loops. By analyzing output from AI systems and comparing it against desired outcomes, businesses can identify discrepancies and adjust input data accordingly. For instance, if an AI tool used for customer service repeatedly misunderstands inquiries about a specific product, noting this trend can lead to refining how related data is fed into the system. It's like course-correcting a ship based on real-world navigation conditions, ensuring the journey stays on track.

Moreover, engaging specialists who focus on data enhancement can be invaluable. These experts bring external perspectives and advanced techniques to help improve datasets. Whether it's using machine learning techniques to augment data or employing domain-specific knowledge to fill gaps, collaborating with professionals skilled in data enrichment can elevate the calibre of available information. Such collaborations can transform a seemingly inadequate dataset into a powerful asset, enabling more intelligent AI applications despite initial constraints.

Determining AI Project Feasibility

Evaluating the viability of an AI project is crucial to ensure it aligns with your organization's objectives and brings tangible benefits. One effective way to do this is by conducting a thorough business needs assessment. This process helps clarify the project's relevance, ensuring it meets the specific requirements of your organization and provides value. It's essential to engage stakeholders during this phase, as their insights can provide valuable perspectives on organizational goals. By involving them early, you not only gain their support but also work towards aligning AI initiatives with broader strategic objectives.

Consider how AI could potentially solve existing issues or enhance current processes within the organization. Are there repetitive tasks that AI can handle more efficiently? Perhaps there's a need for better data analysis capabilities that AI could address. Understanding these specific needs will guide your decision-making and help prioritize AI projects that offer the greatest potential impact.

After identifying relevant business needs, the next step involves conducting a cost-benefit analysis. This step goes beyond just calculating financial implications; it's about understanding the risks involved and evaluating potential returns on investment. In this context, transparent evaluation becomes vital. Transparency fosters trust among stakeholders, making it easier to secure their buy-in. Clearly communicating expected costs, anticipated ROI, and associated risks can reassure stakeholders of the project's validity.

A cost-benefit analysis should encompass both direct and indirect costs. Direct costs might include expenses like software licensing, infrastructure upgrades, or additional personnel. Indirect costs could involve training existing staff or temporarily reallocating resources from other projects. On the benefit side, consider productivity improvements, operational efficiencies, and potential revenue growth stemming from successful AI implementation. Weighing these factors carefully can aid in deciding if the project merits proceeding.

Once you've assessed the needs and conducted a cost-benefit analysis, running pilot programs stands as a pivotal step. Pilots allow organizations to test AI solutions on a smaller scale before full deployment. They serve as testing grounds to identify potential pitfalls and challenges while documenting outcomes that inform future planning. By starting small, it's possible to observe real-world impacts without committing significant resources prematurely.

During a pilot, closely monitor performance metrics to gauge success. Collect data on how effectively the AI solution addresses the identified business needs. Does it lead to time savings? Are error rates reduced? Are customer interactions improved? These insights are invaluable for adjusting strategies and refining approaches before scaling up.

In addition to measuring tangible results, pilots also provide an opportunity to gather user feedback. Employees interacting with AI systems can highlight usability issues, suggesting improvements based on firsthand experiences. Encouraging open communication ensures any concerns get addressed early, ultimately smoothing the path for broader adoption.

Another advantage of pilot programs is that they facilitate learning and adaptation. As you trial different aspects of AI solutions, you'll likely encounter unexpected challenges—technical glitches, integration difficulties, or changes in user behavior. Treat these issues as learning opportunities rather than setbacks. Solving them at this stage minimizes disruptions when rolling out AI across the organization.

Furthermore, documenting outcomes from pilot programs is crucial for ongoing improvement. Maintain detailed records of both successes and failures encountered during the trial phase. Analyze this information to identify trends and patterns that may guide decisions in future AI projects. These lessons learned help build institutional knowledge and improve readiness for subsequent implementations.

Throughout these steps, it's essential to maintain a focus not only on technological advancements but also on human elements. Engage employees in discussions about the project's goals and potential impacts. Address concerns regarding job displacement openly and transparently. Highlight how AI can augment roles rather than replace them entirely, perhaps freeing up time for more strategic activities.

Communicate clearly with all stakeholders, keeping them informed of progress and soliciting input where necessary. This inclusive approach fosters a sense of ownership and collaboration, increasing the likelihood of successful implementation. Remember, humans drive AI technology forward; their involvement and expertise shape its integration into daily operations.

Innovative Solutions to Overcome Resistance

Understanding and embracing change is often seen as a hurdle within organizations looking to adopt new technologies, like artificial intelligence (AI). This resistance can stem from a variety of factors, including fear of the unknown or concerns about job security. To address this resistance effectively, several strategies can be employed, beginning with implementing robust change management frameworks.

Change management frameworks are crucial in any significant organizational transformation, including AI adoption. These frameworks provide structured approaches that facilitate smooth transitions by focusing on effective communication and role clarification. For instance, it's vital for leadership to clearly communicate the benefits and goals of AI integration. Ensuring that all team members understand how AI will enhance operations rather than replace human roles alleviates fears and fosters a sense of inclusion.

In addition to clear communication, defining roles in the context of these changes is essential. Employees need to know exactly how their responsibilities will evolve with the integration of AI into their workflows. This clarification helps reduce uncertainty and enhances job satisfaction, as employees feel more secure about their place in the organization. A well-defined framework also includes feedback mechanisms, allowing staff to express concerns and suggestions, which can help tailor the implementation process to better meet everyone's needs.

One impactful strategy to lower resistance is showcasing success stories. Highlighting cases where AI implementation has been successful within or outside the organization serves multiple purposes. It not only builds trust but also paints a realistic picture of what successful AI adoption looks like. Such stories can show tangible outcomes, such as increased efficiency or improved customer experiences, which resonate with employees' own experiences and aspirations. Celebrating these victories becomes a motivational tool, encouraging stakeholders at all levels to see AI as a valuable ally rather than a threat.

Illustrating real-life examples, especially from peer organizations, can be particularly persuasive. For instance, a retail business might showcase how another company used AI to enhance inventory management, resulting in reduced waste and increased sales. By drawing parallels, employees can visualize similar benefits within their own realms, making the prospect of change less daunting.

Another critical element in overcoming resistance is involving employees early in the process. Forming cross-functional teams can significantly ease the transition to AI by bringing together diverse perspectives and fostering collaboration. Cross-functional teams enable different departments to work together from the start, ensuring that AI solutions align with actual operational needs and challenges rather than being imposed from above.

When employees are involved early on, they have the opportunity to directly contribute to the planning and execution phases, fostering a sense of ownership and empowerment. This inclusivity leads to greater acceptance and enthusiasm for the technology. Additionally, these teams can identify potential roadblocks early and propose practical solutions, leveraging their intimate knowledge of everyday operations.

Training opportunities also play a pivotal role. Offering training sessions and workshops demystifies AI, providing employees with a chance to learn about its capabilities and limitations firsthand. When individuals feel competent in using new tools, their confidence grows, thus reducing fear of inadequacy or obsolescence. Training can range from technical skills development for those directly interacting with AI systems to general awareness sessions for the broader workforce, ensuring everyone feels prepared for the changes.

Moreover, it's beneficial to establish a continuous learning culture where employees are encouraged to develop new skills regularly. This not only aids in adapting to AI but also prepares them for future technological shifts, making the organization more resilient overall. Providing access to both online and in-person training resources ensures accessibility and accommodates different learning styles.

Final Insights

As we wrap up this chapter, let's revisit the roadblocks small organizations face with AI and the practical solutions laid out. From budget constraints to scalability issues, these hurdles can feel daunting. But remember, breaking down investments into manageable phases and choosing cost-effective tools allows even the smallest teams to harness AI's potential without overextending themselves. Emphasizing quality over quantity in your data strategy can also make a significant difference, providing robust training for AI systems despite limited datasets.

Adopting AI isn't just about technology—it's about embracing a cultural shift. Clear communication and hands-on training play a huge role in easing transition anxiety among employees. Encouraging an open dialogue ensures everyone is on board and part of the journey. By setting up pilot programs and celebrating early wins, organizations can build confidence and enthusiasm for future advancements. Integrating AI thoughtfully and inclusively will not only streamline processes but also foster innovation, ensuring that everyone is excited to be part of the change AI brings.

Chapter 18

Embracing an AI-Driven Future

T hinking about our future with AI might seem a bit intimidating, but let's dive into it together. AI is reshaping our world, from how businesses operate to the skills we need for our careers. It's not just a far-off idea; it's happening now, right in front of us. As technology evolves rapidly, staying ahead means continuously adapting and learning. This chapter will explore how embracing these changes, rather than resisting them, can open up exciting opportunities and new ways of living.

We'll be looking at how both individuals and organizations can gear up for an AI-driven world. For individuals, this means keeping skills sharp and learning new ones, while also finding ways to stay resilient amidst tech changes. It's about recognizing that learning never truly ends and failure is just another step on the path to success. On the organizational side, adaptability is essential—companies need to integrate AI in smart ways that encourage collaboration and creativity among teams. This chapter highlights how fostering a culture of openness and cross-functional teamwork can make all the difference. Also, we'll discuss the importance of long-term planning in utilizing AI strategically to identify new markets and innovate effectively. So, let's embark on this journey of understanding how we can embrace AI's potential responsibly and creatively!

The Importance of Maintaining Agility in Adaptation

Adapting to an evolving AI landscape is now more important than ever as technology continues to grow at lightning speed. We're living in a time where artificial intelligence is no longer a distant concept but a part of our daily lives. In this world, the skills we have today might not be enough for tomorrow, and it's crucial to keep updating them. As AI technologies develop, they often bring changes to job roles across various industries. For instance, tasks once done manually are now automated, requiring individuals to learn new skills or risk falling behind.

It's important to embrace skill development as a continuous journey rather than a one-time event. Practical steps like enrolling in online courses, attending workshops, or simply staying informed about AI-related topics can make a significant difference. By actively seeking new learning opportunities and embracing change, we prepare ourselves for a future where AI plays a central role.

For organizations, adaptability means more than just keeping up with technological advancements. It involves rethinking their structures to allow smooth integration of AI innovations. One way to achieve this is by establishing flexible organizational structures that support cross-functional teams. Such setups encourage collaboration between departments, enabling quicker response to AI-driven industry shifts. Take, for example, a retail company using AI to optimize supply chains. A team comprising IT experts, supply chain managers, and data analysts working together would integrate AI solutions more effectively than isolated departments trying to work independently.

Cross-functional teams also promote creativity and problem-solving from multiple perspectives, which is essential in navigating the complexities of AI. Encouraging a culture of collaboration and openness helps organizations remain agile, respond rapidly to change, and seize new opportunities presented by AI developments.

On a personal level, maintaining resilience amid rapid technological changes requires more than just technical skills. Developing practices such as mindfulness can support mental well-being in a constantly evolving environment. Mindfulness, which focuses on being present and aware, aids in managing stress and maintaining focus. These qualities can help individuals cope with the uncertainties and fast pace of AI advancements. Similarly, engaging with communities—whether through professional networks or local groups—offers a support system that fosters shared insights and collective growth.

Community engagement also provides diverse perspectives and experiences, enriching one's understanding of AI's potential impact. By participating in these discussions, we gain awareness of both the benefits and challenges AI might bring, preparing ourselves for future scenarios.

Moreover, long-term planning is a critical component of adapting successfully to an AI-driven future. Incorporating potential AI advancements into strategic plans enables us to anticipate changes and prepare accordingly. This doesn't mean predicting every possible development; rather, it's about considering how AI trends might influence business models, processes, and goals.

An effective approach to long-term planning involves setting aside time to regularly review and adjust strategies based on AI developments and emerging technologies. Organizations that make such planning integral to their operations often find themselves better positioned to capitalize on technological shifts. They can identify new markets, innovate products or services, and pivot when needed—all thanks to foresight grounded in current AI trends.

Emphasizing Lifelong Learning Alongside AI Evolutions

In embracing an AI-driven future, lifelong learning becomes indispensable. With the rapid advancements in artificial intelligence, continuously educating oneself is paramount for understanding and adapting to new developments. As AI evolves, so must our skills and knowledge. This isn't just about keeping our professional lives afloat; it's about thriving in an era where technology is redefining what we can achieve.

For many, ongoing education might feel daunting. However, it doesn't necessarily require formal classroom settings. Online courses, workshops, webinars, and even simple articles or videos can offer substantial updates on AI trends and technologies. These resources allow us to tailor education to our needs, fitting both our schedules and interests. Engaging with these materials helps bridge the gap between current capabilities and future demands, ensuring we remain relevant and competent in an AI-influenced landscape.

As you embark on this journey of continual learning, it's essential to redefine failure. Traditional views cast failure as something negative, but when it comes to learning and growth, failure serves a unique purpose. Each setback, mistake, or wrong turn provides an invaluable learning experience. It forces us to analyze what went wrong and why, setting the stage for deeper understanding and skill enhancement. Viewing failure through this positive lens cultivates resilience and adaptability, helping learners embrace the iterative process that is key to mastering AI-related skills.

Moreover, building a community around learning AI can significantly enrich this experience. Learning is rarely a solitary endeavor; it thrives on interaction, discussion, and shared insights. By connecting with others who are also navigating the complexities of AI, individuals can gain different perspectives and collective wisdom. Community forums, local meetups, and online platforms dedicated to AI discussions can be excellent venues for exchanging ideas and deepening understanding. Such communities provide not only support but also motivation to push further and explore more. They transform isolated efforts into collaborative experiences that multiply learning opportunities and outcomes.

The value of mentorship should not be underestimated in this context. Finding a mentor experienced in AI can offer guidance and open doors to industry knowledge that might otherwise be difficult to access. Mentors can help demystify complex topics, share real-world applications of AI, and provide feedback on one's progress. They act as navigators, assisting in traversing the often-dense landscape of AI. When faced with challenging concepts or decisions, having a mentor to consult can boost confidence and encourage more daring exploration. This relationship not only enhances technical skills but also nurtures softer skills like communication, critical thinking, and strategic planning—essential attributes for anyone looking to make a mark in an AI-driven world.

Yet, for those starting their journey, the concept of lifelong learning might seem overwhelming. The key lies in breaking down goals into manageable steps and celebrating small victories along the way. Setting clear objectives, such as learning a new programming language, understanding a specific AI tool, or staying updated on ethical considerations, makes the learning curve less steep. It's important to remember that lifelong learning is not a sprint but a marathon. The pace and methods will vary for each individual, but the commitment remains consistent: a dedication to continuous improvement and adaptation.

To complement personal endeavors, organizations play a significant role by fostering a culture of experimentation and innovation. Encouraging employees to experiment, take risks, and explore creative solutions fosters an environment where lifelong learning becomes part of the organizational fabric. Guidelines here might include establishing dedicated time for learning, supporting attendance at AI conferences, or developing internal training programs. Such actions demonstrate an organization's commitment to growth and its understanding that employee development is linked to overall success.

Furthermore, cultivating a mindset that values both collaboration and competition within teams can lead to innovative outcomes. By promoting open dialogue and cross-functional collaborations, workplaces thrive on the exchange of diverse ideas. Encouragement to think outside the box and challenge existing norms stimulates creativity, aiding in AI exploration and adoption.

AI as a Priority in Strategic Planning

In today's rapidly evolving technological landscape, integrating AI strategies into planning processes is not just beneficial—it's essential.

As we pivot towards a future increasingly dominated by artificial intelligence, understanding and preparing for its potential impacts becomes a strategic advantage. The ability to anticipate AI's influence on various industries through strategic foresight allows businesses and individuals alike to mitigate risks effectively.

Consider the swift advancements AI has brought to sectors like healthcare, finance, and logistics. These areas have already undergone significant transformation, showcasing both opportunities and challenges. By analyzing trends and projecting future scenarios, organizations can identify potential disruptions and craft strategies that turn these challenges into competitive advantages. For instance, companies in the automotive industry are not only preparing for AI-driven autonomous vehicles but also considering how AI can optimize their manufacturing processes and supply chain management. This proactive approach provides an opportunity to stay ahead of technological shifts and reduce the risk of being caught unprepared by sudden changes.

Aligning operational practices with AI capabilities is another crucial step in this process. Integrating AI tools into everyday operations not only enhances productivity but also heightens organizational readiness. Through automation, data analytics, and machine learning, AI can streamline tasks, allowing human resources to be redirected towards more strategic functions. An example can be seen in customer service departments, where AI chatbots handle routine inquiries, freeing up human agents to focus on complex customer needs. This alignment ensures that businesses remain nimble and capable in an ever-changing environment.

Moreover, prioritizing investments and collaborations centered around AI is vital for securing long-term benefits and fostering innovation. Organizations that allocate resources to develop AI solutions or partner with tech innovators often find themselves on the cutting edge of their respective fields. Investing in AI-driven research and development can lead to breakthroughs that redefine market dynamics and open up new revenue streams. A notable example is the partnership between pharmaceutical companies and AI firms to expedite drug discovery processes, significantly reducing time-to-market for new medications.

Collaboration extends beyond business partnerships; educational institutions also play a critical role. By working together, academic researchers and industry professionals can create a fertile ground for cultivating novel ideas and ethical AI applications. This collective effort not only accelerates technological advancement but also ensures responsible usage of AI technologies.

To sustain momentum in this AI-driven world, regular reviews and stakeholder feedback are indispensable. Navigating the complexities of AI implementation demands continuous reflection and adaptation. Regularly assessing AI strategies against organizational goals allows for timely course corrections and optimization of AI use. Engaging stakeholders in this process ensures diverse perspectives and comprehensive understanding of AI's impact across different areas of business and society.

Stakeholder involvement fosters a culture of accountability, encouraging transparency in AI deployment and boosting public trust. By maintaining open channels of communication and actively listening to feedback from employees, partners, and customers, organizations can address concerns promptly and refine their AI strategies accordingly. This approach cultivates an environment where AI is viewed not as a threat but as a valuable tool for progress.

Additionally, stakeholder engagement provides insights into societal expectations and ethical considerations surrounding AI use. Understanding these dimensions is crucial for developing AI systems aligned with human values and societal norms. Organizations that prioritize ethics in AI strategy not only avert potential backlash but also enhance their brand reputation and attract socially conscious consumers.

As we continue to integrate AI into planning processes, it's essential to view it as an ongoing journey rather than a finite project. The pace of AI evolution necessitates agility and openness to change. By embedding AI strategies into the core of planning, decision-makers are better positioned to harness its full potential, drive operational excellence, and unlock unprecedented opportunities for growth and innovation.

Fostering Partnerships Between Academia and Industry

In the dynamic landscape of artificial intelligence, collaboration stands as one of the pivotal pillars driving ethical and innovative development. As AI technologies continue to advance and reshaping different aspects of our society, it is essential to explore how teamwork between varying sectors can ensure responsible utilization and application.

One profound way collaboration manifests is through joint research endeavors between academia and industry. Universities have long been hubs of knowledge and innovation, with researchers diving deep into theoretical aspects that underpin technological advances. When these academic insights meet the practical needs and resources of the commercial sector, groundbreaking developments occur. This synergy not only fuels innovative AI applications but also ensures that these technologies are crafted with a sense of responsibility towards societal impacts. By working together, academia and industry can develop AI tools that are not only cutting-edge but also aligned with ethical standards and public welfare.

For students about to step into the realm of AI, internship programs play a crucial role in bridging the gap between theoretical learning and practical execution. These programs offer them a firsthand glimpse into real-world challenges, fostering problem-solving skills and understanding the complexities of AI systems. Experiencing such practical scenarios equips students with the knowledge to tackle AI-related issues responsibly. Companies benefit too, as they gain fresh perspectives from budding talents who are eager to innovate. Thus, internships create an invaluable learning loop, promoting growth for both individuals and organizations.

Meanwhile, the academic curriculum itself is evolving to match the rapid pace of AI advancements. Shifts in educational programs now emphasize AI competencies alongside ethical considerations. It's no longer sufficient to understand just the technology; students must grapple with the broader implications of AI decisions. An enriched curriculum that integrates courses on data ethics, algorithmic bias, and AI governance ensures that future professionals are well-rounded and prepared to use AI in ways that respect ethical boundaries. By producing graduates who are technically proficient and ethically mindful, educational institutions contribute significantly to the responsible evolution of AI.

Another key avenue of collaborative success lies in leveraging academic resources and promoting open collaboration platforms. Academic institutions house vast repositories of research, data, and expertise. By opening these resources to wider communities, including independent researchers, startups, and larger corporations, the theoretical ideas can be tested, refined, and implemented with practical feedback. Platforms that encourage this kind of openness foster an environment where theory and practice converge, providing fertile ground for innovation. Open-access journals, shared databases, and collaborative workshops or online forums enable diverse minds to connect, share, and build upon each other's work, ultimately leading to more robust and ethically sound AI outcomes.

To effectively integrate AI advancements into long-term plans, there's a pronounced need for strategies that incorporate potential developments in AI. Long-term planning can ensure preparedness for future shifts, enabling stakeholders to navigate potential challenges efficiently. Encouraging future-oriented thinking in these collaborations can help forecast trends, mitigate risks, and align efforts with responsible innovation. Guidelines stressing the importance of adaptable strategies can provide teams with frameworks to operationalize their AI visions while remaining flexible to changes.

Taking initiative in shaping how AI influences our futures is vital. Active participation in collaborative efforts empowers individuals and organizations to mold AI-driven landscapes conscientiously. Collaborators must engage proactively, seizing opportunities to lead discussions, shape policies, and advocate for AI practices that are sustainable and equitable. By doing so, they not only contribute to immediate advancements but also chart pathways that safeguard societal interests against unforeseen consequences of AI usage.

Ultimately, the symbiotic relationship among academia, industry, and other stakeholders is at the heart of developing AI technologies that are both potent and principled. Each plays a distinct and indispensable role, contributing unique strengths to the collective endeavor. Together, they can navigate the complexities of AI landscapes, creating machines that serve human values and contribute positively to global progress.

Inspiring Responsible AI Use and Attitudes

In today's rapidly evolving technological landscape, fostering a culture of ethical and responsible engagement with AI technology is more critical than ever. As artificial intelligence becomes increasingly integrated into daily life, understanding its ethical implications is essential for promoting fairness and transparency in its use. This discussion needs to be accessible to everyone, not just experts. By doing so, we empower individuals from all walks of life to engage with AI more responsibly.

One key aspect involves comprehending the ethical issues surrounding AI. It's important because AI systems can impact decisions across various sectors—from healthcare to finance—and these decisions must be made fairly. Let's imagine an AI that's used to screen job applicants. If it learns from biased data, those biases carry over, affecting who gets hired. Understanding such implications allows us to advocate for fairness and ensure AI applications are transparent. Advocating for fairness means demanding clarity on how AI systems make decisions. For instance, when selecting candidates or approving loans, transparency ensures that individuals understand why certain choices are made. This understanding helps prevent discrimination and promotes equal opportunities, emphasizing the importance of solid ethical frameworks.

Established ethical frameworks play a crucial role here. These frameworks serve as guiding principles for AI developers, ensuring their creations align with societal values. Various international guidelines exist already, like the European Commission's Ethics Guidelines for Trustworthy AI, which recommend developing AI systems that are lawful, ethical, and robust. Such guidelines help maintain a balance between innovation and responsibility. They encourage developers to consider privacy, accountability, and non-discrimination throughout the AI lifecycle. By embedding these principles into technology from the outset, we create products that respect human rights and dignity.

Moreover, civic engagement plays a pivotal role in shaping public discourse on AI's social implications and policies. Engaging communities in discussions about AI policies enables diverse perspectives to be heard. This engagement can manifest through workshops, public hearings, and online forums where people share concerns and insights. Public participation ensures that policy-making isn't confined to boardrooms but reflects society's actual needs and aspirations. For instance, debates on autonomous vehicles often involve input from city planners, residents, transportation officials, and tech companies, aiming to craft regulations that benefit all.

Additionally, sharing positive AI stories is vital to demonstrating successful and ethical applications that benefit communities. Highlighting these examples dispels fears about AI being solely disruptive or dangerous. Take, for example, AI-driven tools that assist doctors in diagnosing diseases faster or more accurately. Stories like these showcase AI's potential to enhance human ability and improve lives. Another inspiring example comes from agriculture, where AI technologies optimize crop yields and reduce waste. By showcasing such success stories, we illustrate the tangible benefits of adopting AI ethically.

Encouraging literacy in AI ethics within educational programs is also an avenue worth exploring. While this chapter focuses on fostering ethical behavior, planting seeds early in academic curricula builds a foundation for future generations dedicated to responsible AI development. Schools and universities could introduce basic courses discussing AI's societal impacts, encouraging students to think critically about the technology they might one day help create. Providing real-world case studies and inviting industry professionals to speak at events can further bridge gaps between theoretical learning and practical application.

Furthermore, partnerships between public entities, private organizations, academia, and civil society can strengthen efforts toward ethical AI implementation. Collaboration between different stakeholders brings together varied expertise, promoting more comprehensive solutions tailored towards public welfare. For instance, tech companies partnering with non-governmental organizations (NGOs) focused on digital rights can lead to innovative projects that extend internet access while respecting user privacy. These collaborations highlight how collective efforts yield more balanced outcomes than isolated initiatives.

As we continue to explore the vast possibilities presented by AI, maintaining open dialogues about potential challenges remains paramount. Balancing optimism about technological advancements with realistic assessments ensures societies remain vigilant against unintended consequences. This vigilance relies heavily on the participation of informed citizens actively engaged in discussions around ethics and policy. It encourages continuous learning, driven by curiosity rather than fear, fostering environments where questions are valued as much as answers.

Final Insights

As we close this chapter, remember that embracing the future of AI is about being proactive and flexible. We've talked about the importance of keeping our skills fresh and learning continuously. It's not just about getting through today's tasks but gearing up for what tomorrow might bring. The world of AI is evolving fast, and staying curious helps us keep up. Whether it's signing up for a short course or joining a local tech meet-up, every little step counts. On a personal level, things like mindfulness can help manage the stress of constant change, acting as mental boosts in this fast-paced environment.

On a broader scale, fostering collaboration within organizations is key to thriving in an AI-driven world. By encouraging departments to work together and creating opportunities for cross-functional teams, we can better harness AI's potential. Such teamwork leads to innovative solutions by blending diverse insights and skills. In the end, it's all about anticipating changes and adapting wisely. Being open to new ideas and having a plan in place prepares us to capitalize on AI advancements while ensuring ethical and responsible usage. This journey isn't just a challenge; it's an exciting chance to grow both personally and professionally as we build a future with AI.

Conclusion

T hroughout this journey, we've explored the fascinating world of artificial intelligence, tracing its development from early imaginings to the powerful presence it holds in our lives today. We've learned that AI is more than just algorithms and data; it's a transformative force reshaping industries, enhancing how we interact with technology, and altering the landscape of daily life. By understanding AI's foundations, applications, and potential impacts, you've equipped yourself with the knowledge to navigate this dynamic field confidently.

For many, the idea of AI can provoke mixed feelings—excitement tempered with apprehension. It's perfectly natural to feel a sense of uncertainty about a rapidly evolving technology that seems both exciting and intimidating. But as we've seen throughout this guide, AI is fundamentally a tool—a tool designed to empower us, enhance creativity, streamline efficiencies, and solve complex problems. It's important to recognize that AI isn't here to replace humanity but to complement and enhance what we do. When used responsibly, AI has the potential to enrich our lives and address challenges that were once thought insurmountable.

Consider the remarkable ways AI is already aiding medical diagnostics, optimizing resource management, personalizing education, and enhancing communication. These advancements are not only creating new opportunities but are also paving the way for solutions to global issues such as healthcare accessibility, environmental sustainability, and more precise educational methods. The overarching message is clear: AI, when harnessed ethically and thoughtfully, can be a force for good in society.

It's crucial to address the concerns and skepticism some may have about AI's role in our future. Questions surrounding privacy, job displacement, and ethical considerations are valid and must be taken seriously. But rather than view these challenges as barriers, consider them as catalysts for dialogue and innovation. Embracing AI doesn't mean accepting it unquestioningly but rather engaging with it critically. By actively participating in conversations about AI's direction and application, we can help steer its development towards outcomes that align with shared human values.

One of the key takeaways from this book is the importance of ongoing education regarding AI. The pace of technological change is relentless, and staying informed is your best defense against being left behind. As AI evolves, so should our understanding of it—and that means continuing to learn. This book serves as merely the opening chapter of your lifelong learning journey in the realm of artificial intelligence. Whether through online courses, workshops, or community discussions, the resources available are vast and varied. Keep exploring, questioning, and expanding your horizons.

The dialogue around AI is one in which all voices matter, including yours. We find ourselves at a critical juncture where the integration of AI into society presents enormous potential and responsibility. Engage actively in these discussions, advocate for ethical practices, and consider yourself part of the conversation. By being proactive rather than reactive, you can influence how AI technologies are adopted and integrated into your field of interest.

Imagine a future where AI democratizes access to information, bridges gaps in healthcare, reduces inefficiencies in energy consumption, and fosters inclusivity in digital spaces. This optimistic vision requires collective effort, guided by empathy and driven by innovation. Being informed and involved means you're not just watching these changes unfold from the sidelines; you're helping shape an AI-driven future that reflects our best intentions and aspirations.

As we conclude, reflect on the vast possibilities that lie ahead. The narrative around AI is still being written, and each one of us has a role to play in its unfolding story. Whether you're a professional seeking to enhance your career, a skeptic searching for balanced perspectives, or a curious learner ready to dive deeper into AI, remember that every step you take contributes to a broader understanding and better implementation of this transformative technology.

Thank you for embarking on this journey through the pages of this book. May your newfound insights inspire you to continue exploring, questioning, and shaping the future of AI. Let this be not the end, but merely the beginning of a lifelong engagement with one of the most significant technological advances of our time. With curiosity as your guide and knowledge as your ally, step forward into the burgeoning world of AI with confidence and optimism.

www.ingramcontent.com/pod-product-compliance
Lightning Source LLC
LaVergne TN
LVHW051333050326
832903LV00031B/3523